JOURNAL OF QUALITY ASSURANCE FOR HIGHER EDUCATION INSTITUTIONS IN MALAWI

Book II

Kingstone Ngwira

authorHOUSE®

AuthorHouse™
1663 Liberty Drive
Bloomington, IN 47403
www.authorhouse.com
Phone: 1 (800) 839-8640

Published by AuthorHouse 01/08/2016

ISBN: 978-1-5049-6973-4 (sc)
ISBN: 978-1-5049-6974-1 (e)

Abstract

Higher Education is considered to play a unique role in all parts of the world. Quality Assur- ance in Higher Education is more complicated than quality assurance in industry because there are so many players in the field. For example Higher Education has many stakeholders such as Government or the State, Employers, Academic World, Students, Parents, Society at Large and all stakeholders have their own ideas and needs. This is a call to address the issue of quality in the university education provision. This effort should be pursued in response to the realization of the importance that development of human resources through Quality Assurance in higher education is harmonized. Well established higher education institutions in the USA, Europe, Africa and other parts of the world have defined quality as input (students, staff, facilities), quality of process (teaching and learning) and outputs (graduates, results on research and consultancies). There is need for Higher Education Institutions to produce quality research products since quality output of institutions does not only come through delivery of curricula but also from quality research products. This is an area of Higher Education Sector that needs to be redressed. Therefore Higher Education Institutions need to build capacity in this area through Postgraduate training and collaborative approach to research proposal writing and implementation. Research Collaboration will contribute to both knowledge generation and exchange and also capacity building for supporting institutional development and promote global integration. The on-going process to develop quality assurance framework and the future Higher Education Institutions as a common Higher Educational Area is paramount. This will require process of internal and external program assessment in Higher Education Institutions as an integration of tracer study (graduate survey) into quality assurance and management processes in Higher Education Institutions

Introduction

In recent years universities in developing countries have followed their counterparts in developed countries in adopting quality assurance to improve the quality of their teaching, research and direct community service programmes. While many of the conditions required for the successful implementation of quality assurance programmes are not present in most universities in developing countries, their adoption will still be useful. Such programmes show how a university's seemingly disparate activities are related to one another to serve a common cause and how the quality of these can best be improved by adopting an integrated approach. In the process, they provide more focus and direction to the work of the traditional academic committee system. However, the quality assurance programmes must be modified to suit the conditions prevailing in developing countries, by being simple in design, modest in expectations, and realistic in requirements

Higher Education is considered to play a unique role in Malawi and this is because of the history of university education in both the public and private universities. Many Universities have been established and National Council of Higher Education (NCHE) in Malawi has registered an upward trend in its membership from where Credentials and Evaluation Committee left and the number is expected to increase significantly with many Universities applying for registration.

Based on this growth or increase the effort to harmonise quality assurance in higher education institutions in Malawi is paramount. This effort is being pursued in response to the realization of the importance of the higher education to the Malawi economy on one hand and the evolving multiple stakeholders' community on the other. It is therefore of great importance that the development of human resources through quality assurance is higher education in Malawi is harmonised. To this end I would like to acknowledge the role played by NCHE in Malawi for guidance in the development of this book.

Quality assurance in higher education is by no means only a Malawian concern. All over the world there is an increasing interest in quality and standards, reflecting both the rapid growth of higher education and its cost to the public and the private purse. Accordingly, if Malawi is to achieve its aspiration to be the most dynamic and knowledge-based economy in the world, then higher education in Malawi will need to demonstrate that it takes the quality of its programmes and awards seriously and is willing to put into place the means of assuring and demonstrating that quality. The initiatives and demands, which are springing up both inside and outside Malawi in the face of this internationalisation of higher education, demand a response.

This book on Quality Assurance for Higher Education Institutions in Malawi is a Road Map to Quality. Quality Assurance (QA) may have different definitions but the basic idea is that higher education institutions must convince all stakeholders that they are doing paramount efforts to pre- pare young people and people of all ages to fit their communities and to lead productive lives.

Among other things the book has highlighted issues such as guidelines for self assessment at program level aims at the faculty/department to learn more about the quality of the programs by means of an effective self assessment, guidelines for external assessment explains the procedures and pro- cesses for an external evaluation at program level.

The specific target group is the external expert team, but also the faculty/department to be assessed, guidelines for self - assessment at institutional level aims especially at the central management of an institution and offers an instrument to discover more about the quality and the institution. The implementation of a Quality Assurance system aims at all levels of an institution, but especially useful for the Quality Assurance coordinators for the development and installation of an Internal Quality Assurance (IQA) system. External Quality Assurance for higher education institutions in Malawi provides the reader with the background information about the state-of-the-art in external quality assurance systems for higher education in Malawi and discusses the role of the regulatory bodies such as National Council for higher education (NCHE) in the light of national higher education development.

The book also aims to support the higher education institutions in Malawi in: Implementing good practices for quality assurance; Applying the standards and criteria, as formulated by competent authorities; developing an adequate IQA system that fits national and international developments; discovering their own quality by offering self-assessment instruments for IQA and the teaching/learning process, and for some institutional aspects.

The current volume, Guidelines for Assessment at program level offers the faculties/ departments a tool to carry out the assessment-assessment and to prepare for external assessment. The book is written in a broad and general approach. However, the tool has to be adapted to the specific situation of the Universities and specific situation at faculty/department. The content is based on experiences and good practices from all over the world. Universities should look at what is going on internationally, while developing internal quality assurance mechanisms. At the same time, universities cannot neglect the developments at national, regional and in different countries.

Quest for excellence and learner satisfaction represents an historic commitment and foundation of important higher education milestones relating to Quality and Accountability. In the medieval age, universities were dedicated to the spirit of learning, nowadays, they need to cover not only learning, but also research and entrepreneurial activities. This expansion of activities reveals the need to develop Quality Management (QM). Quality Management aims to develop a "Quality Cul- ture" where Quality is seen as everyone's responsibility.

The three spheres of Quality Management activities are: Quality Planning, Quality Control and Quality Assurance. Quality Planning selects applicable procedures or standards for a particular objective. Quality control ensures that they are followed. A common language among various higher education systems facilitates the understanding of quality concepts. In this book, I have used the Quality Assurance standards for higher education in Malawi to discover the basics in Quality Assurance, with emphasis on the internal Quality Assurance in higher education institutions.

Concept of Quality

The concept of quality assurance (QA) is not new. Many experienced professionals have writ- ten numerous books on this area. However, research has shown that books written in this area are largely meant to meet the needs of human resource acquisitioned in Quality Assurance. This means that for those that are not professionals in the field but still desire to have a knowledge of quality assurance the need to fill the gap does exist. This book is written to fill that gap existing in the quality assurance literature.

There are different approaches to quality assurance. The meaning of quality assurance may vary depending on the field of activity. Different countries have evolved quality assurance models for their higher education systems as necessitated by their unique national context. Nevertheless, in all activities related to quality assurance across the world, there lies a common unifying thread that laces together the basic concepts. This book discusses the current quality assurance vocabulary, the prominent modes and different practices.

Broader access to higher education is an opportunity for higher education institutions to make use of increasingly diverse individual experiences. Responding to diversity and growing expectations for higher education requires a fundamental shift in its provision; it requires a more student-centred approach to learning and teaching, embracing flexible learning paths and recognising competences gained outside formal curricula. Higher education institutions themselves also become more diverse in their missions, mode of educational provision and cooperation, including growth of internationalisation, digital learning and new forms of delivery. The role of quality assurance is crucial in supporting higher education systems and institutions in responding to these changes while ensuring the qualifications achieved by students and their experience of higher education re- main at the forefront of institutional missions.

A key goal of the Standards and Guidelines for Quality Assurance in the Higher Education Area is to contribute to the common understanding of quality assurance for learning and teaching across borders and among all stakeholders. They have played and will continue to play an important role in the development of national and institutional quality assurance systems across the Malawi Higher Education Area and cross-border cooperation. Engagement with quality assurance processes, particularly the external ones, allows higher education systems to demonstrate quality and increase transparency, thus helping to build mutual trust and better recognition of their qualifications, programmes and other provision.

This book has been written with four objectives. First, to raise general awareness of quality assurance in higher education institutions in Malawi. Second, to develop quality assessment competencies for higher education institutions in Malawi. Third, to promote a culture of quality in higher education institutions in Malawi. Fourth, to support the efforts of National Council for Higher Education (NCHE) in providing accreditation and quality assurance services in higher education institutions in Malawi.

According to NCHE (2014) The National Council for Higher Education (NCHE) was established by Act of Parliament No. 15 of 2011, with the primary purpose of providing accreditation and quality assurance services in higher education institutions. Specifically, the NCHE aims to promote and coordinate education provided by higher education institutions, design quality assurance systems and determine, maintain and regulate standards for teaching, examinations, qualifications and facilities; register, de-register and accredit higher education institutions; determine framework for funding higher education and provide guidance on terms and conditions for awarding students' grants, loans and scholarships; and harmonize student selection into public higher education institutions.

National Council for Higher Education has the following functions: Promote and co-ordinate education provided by higher education institutions; Register and de-register higher education institutions; Determine a framework for funding of public higher education institutions; Harmonize selection of students to public universities; Regulate, determine and maintain standards of teaching, examinations, academic qualifications, academic facilities; Accredit higher education institutions both public and private; Design and recommend an institutional quality assurance system for higher education; Approve terms and conditions for awarding grants and scholarships to students of higher education institutions and advise the Minister on all matters of Higher Education (NCHE 2014).

It is hoped that the reader will find the contents not only academically enriching but also practical value in their pursuit.

CONTEXT, SCOPE, PURPOSES AND PRINCIPLES

Setting the context

The National Council for Higher Education (NCHE) in Malawi was established to act as the body for scrutinising national qualifications, registering institutions and approving academic programmes for higher education in Malawi. NCHE has established guidelines to assist providers of higher education in designing quality assurance procedures for academic purposes (NCHE 2014)

Higher education, research and innovation play a crucial role in supporting social cohesion, economic growth and global competitiveness. Given the desire for Malawi higher education institutions to become increasingly knowledge-based, higher education is an essential component of socio-economic and cultural development. At the same time, an increasing demand for skills and competences requires higher education to respond in new ways.

NCHE (2014) supports the above views by pointing out that all over the world there is in- creasing interest in higher education quality and standards, reflecting both the rapid growth of higher education and its cost to the public and the private purse. There is a quest for harmonisation of quality higher education in the SADC region. Accordingly, if Malawi is to achieve its aspiration to be a dynamic and knowledge-based economy, then its higher education sector will need to demonstrate that it takes seriously the quality of its programmes and awards and is willing to put in place the means of assuring and demonstrating that quality (NCHE 2014).

Quality assurance in higher education has become a key component in the delivery of education in almost all countries in the world since this affects standards. Most institutions of higher education globally are now aiming at internationalisation of their programmes, which can be done if the standards are acceptable to all stakeholders. Malawi is no exception to the quest for quality assurance, and this need is demonstrated by the public debate on the quality of education.

Broader access to higher education is an opportunity for higher education institutions to make use of increasingly diverse individual experiences. Responding to diversity and growing expectations for higher education requires a fundamental shift in its provision; it requires a more student-centred approach to learning and teaching, embracing flexible learning paths and recognising competences gained outside formal curricula. Higher education institutions themselves also become more diverse in their missions, mode of educational provision and cooperation, including growth of internationalisation, digital learning and new forms of delivery. The role of quality assurance is crucial in supporting higher education systems and institutions in responding to these changes while ensuring the qualifications achieved by students and their experience of higher education re- main at the forefront of institutional missions.

A key goal of the Standards and Guidelines for Quality Assurance in higher education institu- tions in Malawi is to contribute to the common understanding of quality assurance for learning and teaching across borders and among all stakeholders. They are currently playing and will continue to play an important role in the development of national and institutional quality assurance systems across the higher education. Engagement with quality assurance processes, particularly the external ones, allows Malawi higher education systems to demonstrate quality and increase transparency, thus helping to build mutual trust and better recognition of their qualifications, programmes and other provision.

Scope and Concepts

The standards and guidelines for internal and external quality assurance in higher education in Malawi are not standards for quality, nor do they prescribe how the quality assurance processes are implemented, but they provide guidance, covering the areas which are vital for successful quality provision and learning environments in higher education.

The focus of the standards and guidelines is on quality assurance related to learning and teaching in higher education, including the learning environment and relevant links to research and innovation. In addition institutions have policies and processes to ensure and improve the quality of their other activities, such as research and governance.

Higher education aims to fulfill multiple purposes; including preparing students for active citizenship, for their future careers (e.g. contributing to their employability), supporting their personal development, creating a broad advanced knowledge base and stimulating research and innovation. Therefore, stakeholders, who may prioritise different purposes, can view quality in higher education differently and quality assurance needs to take into account these different perspectives. Quality, whilst not easy to define, is mainly a result of the interaction between teachers, students and the institutional learning environment. Quality assurance should ensure a learning environment in which the content of programmes, learning opportunities and facilities are fit for purpose.

At the heart of all quality assurance activities are the twin purposes of accountability and enhancement. Taken together, these create trust in the higher education institutions performance. A successfully implemented quality assurance system will provide information to assure the higher education institution and the public of the quality of the higher education institutions activities (accountability) as well as provide advice and recommendations on how it might improve what it is doing (enhancement). Quality assurance and quality enhancement are thus inter-related. They can support the development of a quality culture that is embraced by all: from the students and academic staff to the institutional leadership and management.

The term „quality assurance" is used in this document to describe all activities within the con- tinuous improvement cycle (i.e. assurance and enhancement activities).

Unless otherwise specified, in the document stakeholders are understood to cover all actors within an institution, including students and staff, as well as external stakeholders such as employ- ers and external partners of an institution.

The word institution is used in the standards and guidelines to refer to higher education institutions. Depending on the institutions approach to quality assurance it can, however, refer to the institution as whole or to any actors within the institution.

Purposes and principles

The Malawian Standards and guidelines for quality assurance advocated by NCHE have the following purposes: They set a common framework for quality assurance systems for learning and teaching at national and institutional level; more importantly they enable the assurance and improvement of quality of higher education in Malawi. Additionally, the guidelines are underpinned by the following principles: programmes should address the interests of students, employers and the society more generally through good quality higher education; international autonomy is critically important, tempered by a recognition that this brings with it heavy responsibilities and external quality assurance has to place only an appropriate and necessary burden on institutions for the achievement of their objectives.

NCHE 2014) mentions that the guidelines quality assurance in higher education must be un- derpinned by the following three fundamental principles: first, programmes should address the in- terests of students, employers, and the society more generally through good quality higher education. Second, institutional autonomy is critically important, tempered by a recognition that this brings with it heavy responsibilities. Third, external quality assurance has to be fit for purpose and to place only an appropriate and necessary burden on institutions for the achievement of their objectives.

Higher Education and Quality Assurance: the first link

The increasing demands for good quality higher education by students and society imply that Higher Educational Institutions (HEI's) now face similar pressures that the business sector has been facing for decades. These implications often become even more serious for HEI's who lack the finance and infrastructure resources and have recognition issues, as well as facing stronger competition from local, distance and international education institutions. Some of the lessons to be learnt from industry are as follows:

- Make the desire for quality an overarching principle in every operation (creating a quality culture)
- Be knowledgeable about the needs of students and academics (the actors involved in the service)
- Creating desirability for the HEI through meeting social and economical trends while maintaining high level of academic integrating and superior quality.

Organisations that provide quality and value in the provision of their educational services are likely to grow and prosper. Such organisations gain benefits like stronger student and staff loyalty, lower vulnerability to economic changes, ability to command higher funding and more autonomy from the state in policy development. Some HEI's currently experience problems in retaining both academic staff and dealing with growing student needs. Some of the reasons for this may be that staff and students perceive that other institutions are offering more valuable education in terms of quality (recognition, career development, student support etc).

It thus, becomes imperative for HEI's to ensure that their services are in demand. Various strategies to make higher education affordable and valuable for students need to be applied on the national level in order to support the social role of the HEI's and the growth in QA methodologies and the implementation of the results of QA both institutional and socially.

Quality Assurance in Higher Education

"An examination of a knife would reveal that its distinctive quality is to cut, and from this we can conclude that a good knife would be a knife that cuts well". Aristotle.

A new form of Quality Assurance

The application of QA in the sphere of Higher Education, while having the same base objectives of defining and recognising quality, is somewhat complicated by the important socio-economic role that education plays in developing local, national and global societies. Quality is the distinguishing characteristic guiding students and higher education institutions when receiving and providing higher education. The integration of Quality Assurance principles into higher education have become a Malawian wide issue since the need for a clear QA and Accreditation system was laid out as one of the aims of NCHE. This move towards integrating QA into higher education has benefited institutions and students by setting out to achieve a model in the international cooperation in higher education, which improves the quality, transparency and comparability of degrees, and studies that have been involved in the process. The benefits that can be gained therefore by having a recognised quality assurance process at a course, faculty, institutional and national level is clear for the institutions and students, academics and society.

Defining Quality Assurance in Higher Education

Quality is often described as the totality of features and characteristics of a service that bear on its ability to satisfy stated or implied needs. Quality in higher education, according to Article 11 of the World Declaration on Higher Education published by the United Nations, is a multi- dimensional concept, which should embrace all its functions and activities: teaching and academic programmes, research and scholarship, staffing, students, buildings, faculties, equipment, services the community and the academic environment. It should take the form of internal self-evaluation and external review, conducted openly by independent specialists, if possible with international expertise, which are vital for enhancing quality. Independent national bodies should be established and comparative standards of quality, recognised at international level, should be defined.

Due attention should be paid to the specific institutional, national and regional contexts in order to take into account diversity and to avoid uniformity. Stakeholders should be an integral part of the institutional evaluation process. Quality also requires that higher education should be characterised by its international dimension: exchange of knowledge, interactive networking, mobility of teachers and students, and international research projects, while taking into account the national cultural values and circumstances.

Principles of QA in Education Aristotle stated in his Book VIII of Politics that „this education and these studies exist for their own sake". In this context quality assurance should exist alongside and support the ideal of „fitness for propose of education" where the purpose is the development of society and education of the individual. Again, there are the two approaches that can be taken to quality assurance, which can define the methods and type of QA processes that higher education institutions can combine:

The intrinsic qualities of higher education refer to the basic values and ideals, which form the very heart of higher education: the unfettered search for truth and the disinterested pursuit of knowledge. It focuses on the knowledge creating processes and student learning. Even though most academics today will agree that quality in higher education is more than this, intrinsic quality rep- resents the core of academic quality. The academic community can be seen as guardians of intrinsic quality.

The extrinsic qualities refer to the capacities of higher education institutions to respond to the changing needs of the society with whom they interact. Extrinsic quality concerns the demands that society directs towards higher education. These demands change in tandem with social changes, which occur over time. It could be argued to what extent extrinsic quality should be determined by economic demands or the state (government) demands - both of which form pillars of society.

This therefore leads to a wider range of issues such as: The purpose of education? The ways in which educational institutions serve society and who decides this? The complex processes of teaching and learning and their evaluation? The development of appropriate knowledge, skills, competencies among staff to enable them to enhance their performance as teachers.

The Quality Assurance of Higher Education in Malawi

Quality In Higher Education is often defined as "fitness for purpose," but there is no agreement on a precise definition of the term. The terms most used to describe quality include quality assurance, quality control, quality audit, quality assessment and academic standards. These definitions have been borrowed as the basis for discussion in the framework. Accordingly, the meaning of the terms as they will be used in the framework are:

Definitions in Quality Assurance

In any discussion about quality assurance in higher education it is clearly important to start by defining the terms and phrases that will be used. The following definitions are the commonly accepted ones and should be a useful point of reference for remainder of this book. Some terms related to quality defined by ESIB (2010) are presented below.

Quality

'Fitness for purpose' - Juran „Conformance to requirements" - Crosby An educational definition is that of an ongoing process ensuring the delivery of agreed standards. These agreed standards should ensure that every educational institution where quality is assured has the potential to achieve a high quality of content and results.

Quality Assurance

The means by which an institution can guarantee with confidence and certainty, that the standards and quality of its educational provision are being maintained and enhanced.

Quality Control

Quality control refers to the verification procedures (both formal and informal) used by institutions in order to monitor quality and standards to a satisfactory standard and as intended.

Quality Enhancement

Quality Enhancement is the process of positively changing activities in order to provide for a continuous improvement in the quality of institutional provision.

Quality Assessment

Quality Assessment is the process of external evaluation undertaken by an external body of the quality of educational provisions in institutions, in particular the quality of the student experience.

Quality Audit

Quality Audit is the process of examining institutional procedures for assuring quality and standards and whether the arrangements are implemented effectively and achieve stated objectives.

The underlying purpose of Continuation Audit is "to establish the extent to which institutions are discharging effectively their responsibilities for the standards of awards granted in their name and for the quality of education provided to enable students to attain standards."

Standards

Standards describe levels of attainment against which performance may be measured. Attainment of a standard usually implies a measure of fitness for a defined purpose.

Quality Culture

Quality Culture is the creation of a high level of internal institutional quality assessment mechanisms and the ongoing implementation of the results. Quality Culture can be seen as the ability of the institution, program etc to develop quality assurance implicitly in the day to day work of the institution and marks a move away form periodic assessment to ingrained quality assurance.

Accreditation

Accreditation is the result of a review of an education program or institution following certain quality standards agreed on beforehand. It's a kind of recognition that a program or institution fulfils certain standards.

The word quality is often used without explaining what quality is. However, everybody who thinks about quality and quality assurance is faced with the question:

"What is Quality?" When talking about quality and quality assurance, it is important to speak the same language. We must understand each other and we must have a shared idea about quality. In this section, some general ideas about quality and quality assurance will be explained.

So What is Quality?

Many discussions on quality start with a quote from the book "Zen and the Art of Motorcycle Maintenance". Quality you know what it is, yet you don't know what it is they have more quality. But when you try to say what quality is, apart from the things that have it, it all goes poof! There's nothing to talk about. But for practical purposes it really does exist. What else are the grades based on? Why else would people pay fortunes for some things and throw others in the trash pile? Obviously some things mental wheels and nowhere finding any place to get traction. What the hell is Quality? What is it?"

In spite of these reflection by Pirsig, many books and articles have been written to try to describe the nature of quality. An absolute definition of quality does not exist because just like beauty quality is in the eyes of the beholder. While the general concept of quality is a difficult one in itself, quality in higher education is much more complex, because it is not always clear what the "product" is and who the "client" is. Is the "graduate" the "product" that we offer society and the labour market? Or is the graduate-to-be, the student, our "client" and the program that we offer the "product"? We can only say that a University has a multiple product system and a multi-client sys- tem.

Quality Assurance in Higher Education is more complicated than quality assurance in indus- try because there are so many players in the field. Higher Education has many stakeholders and all stakeholders have their own ideas and needs. We can distinguish the following stakeholders in Higher Education:

- ☐ Government or the State
- ☐ Employers
- ☐ Academic World

- ☐ Students
- ☐ Parents
- ☐ Society at Large

The concept "quality" is very complex. We can't speak of the quality in Higher Education, but we have to speak about qualities. On one hand, we have to make a distinction between quality requirements set by the different stakeholders: Government or the State; Employers; Academic World; Students; Parents and Society at Large. Each stakeholder will appreciate different aspects of quality. On the other hand quality is not a simple one-dimension notion. Quality is a multidi- mensional. So there is quality input (students, staff, facilities), quality of process (teaching and learning) and outputs (graduates, results on research and consultancies).

All these dimensions have to be taken into account when discussing quality and judging quality. The different views on quality and the multi-dimensional notion of quality mean that it is a waste of time to try to precisely define it. Absolute or objective quality does not exist. However, if we take our quality seriously and if we seriously try to answer our quality we have to agree on a workable concept of quality. Taking into account that each player has his or her own ideas about quality, we can agree that we should try to find a definition of quality that fits most of the ideas and that covers most of the stakeholder expectations.

With so many stakeholders and players in the field, it is not easy to find a definition of qualitybecause stakeholders have their own ideas and expectations. We may therefore say that quality is a matter of negotiation between the academic institution and the stakeholders. In this negotiation process, each stakeholder needs to formulate as clearly as possible, his/ her requirements. The University or faculty as the ultimate supplier of service must try to reconcile all these different wishes and requirements. Sometimes the expectations will run parallel but they can just end up in conflict.

As far as possible, the requirements of all stakeholders should be translated into the mission and goals of an the University and into the objectives of a faculty and the educational program and as far as this concerns research and research programs. The challenge is to achieve the goals, objectives, strategies, and learning outcomes. If this is the case, then we can say that the University, the faculty or department has quality. Figure 3.1 below summarises the quality assurance process.

As said earlier absolute definition of quality does not exist. For the sake of a common understanding, the following descriptions of quality have been adopted. Quality is achieving our goals and aims in an efficient and effective way assuming that the goals and aims reflect the requirements of all our stakeholders in an adequate way. However, talking about quality we have to take into account the following remarks:

Quality is not always the same as efficiency

The discussion of quality assessment is often connected with the concept of "efficiency" (saving money, making more rational use of public resources). In assessing quality, an important question will be: "Do we achieve the required level of quality at acceptable cost?" An efficient oriented approach as such a good starting point but the problem is that efficiency is not always defined as "at acceptable cost" but often as at "minimal cost" and this may threaten quality. For example it may be very efficient to have lecturers for a thousand students but is not effective. It may be considered efficient to have a very structured degree program with student assessments every four weeks, forcing students to work and keep up with the program.

However, does this method lead to the creation of the "right" independent and critically thinking graduate? It may be considered efficient to use only multiple-choice questions for student assessment, but does it enhance verbal and written communication skills?

Quality is Context Bound

When striving for quality, the main question is: "Do we offer the stakeholders what we promise to offer." This means that the starting point for judging quality will be our promises. Therefore we have to look at our quality in the given context. McDonald's, for example we will strive for quality and when we eat a fast food meal, we will probably get quality. If the University claims excellence other criteria count as posed to when the

University's aspiration is to contribute to the development of the country and the region.

Criteria and Standards

Having accepted a workable definition of quality, there is another hot topic how do we assess the quality? How do we measure the quality? What are the criteria for measuring quality? What are the standards against which quality is assessed? If we look at what is said about quality, it becomes obvious that it is impossible to identify one set of criteria or acceptable standards for the quality of higher education. The parties concerned will have their own criteria and norms derived from their own objectives and or demands. This means that the government will formulate other criteria than an employer will do. It is impossible to formulate general criteria for higher education in advance. They will differ from discipline to discipline and stakeholder to stakeholder. The expectations for the labour market will play a totally different role when assessing arts as opposed to electrical engineering, for example. So what is acceptable as quality is a matter of opinion.

Looking for our quality, there are three basic questions:

1. Are we doing the right things? (Checking our goals and aims)
2. Are we doing the right things in the right way? (Thus are in control of the process to achieve our goals and aims?)
3. Do we achieve our goals? (Checking our outcomes)

For assessing our quality, we need a yardstick or benchmark. An absolute yardstick, ready for use does not exist. This means that the institution has to look for criteria and standards that can be used. In some cases the criteria and standards are formulated by one of the stakeholders. The Government for example has formulated criteria and standards in the framework of accreditation. In other cases employers or the profession have formulated standards. When there are no preformulated requirements it is up to PLU to decide upon the standards, taking into account into international developments (benchmarking).

The quest for quality is not an easy one, especially since there is no absolute quality or objective quality. Nevertheless, we expect higher education to assure its quality, to demonstrate its quality and to have its quality assessed by outsiders such as National Council for Higher Education.

Quality Assurance

Quality assurance is the mechanism put in place to guarantee that the education is "fit for purpose" i.e. is good. Every higher education institution must have appropriate and effective internal structure and mechanisms for monitoring its institution quality control procedures to ensure quality.

Quality Control

Quality control is the process of ensuring compliance with standards and procedures set to maintain and enhance quality. For the past 15 years, quality control has not been a satisfactory way of ensuring quality but is seen as an end - of - process solution, the business of quality controllers rather than the responsibility of all stakeholders.

Quality Audit

Audit, in the context of quality in higher education or examining what goes on an institution to ensure that there is institutional compliance with quality assurance procedures, integrity, standards and outcomes.

Quality Assessment

This entails external assessment by peers of the quality of teaching and learning through the scrutiny of institutional documentation and student work by direct observation, interview, as well as reference to performance indicators.

Academic Standards

These are explicit levels of academic attainment used to describe and measure academic requirements and achievements of individual students or group of students. The responsibility of assuring quality lies with each individual institution in partnership with National Council of Higher Education (NCHE), the statutory regulatory authority for higher education in Malawi. For this reason, each institution is required to have a Quality Assurance Unit at the department, faculty and at the central institutional level to address quality issues.

According to NCHE (2014) version 1.0 on Standards and Guidelines for Quality Assurance in Malawi's Higher Education Institutions the National Council for Higher Education was established by Act of Parliament No. 15 of 2011, with the primary purpose of providing accreditation and quality assurance services in higher education institutions. Prior to the establishment of the NCHE, from 1993, accreditation and quality assurance services were provided to new higher education in- stitutions by the Government of Malawi, through the Credentials and Evaluation Committee (CEC). Up until 1993, there was only one public university, the University of Malawi, which was responsible for accrediting new public and private universities and ensuring the quality of their programmes.

NCHE (2014) points out that its key functions are related specifically to quality assurance and accreditation are: to promote and coordinate education provided by higher education institutions; to register and deregister higher education institutions; to regulate, determine and maintain standards of teaching, examinations, academic qualifications, academic facilities; to accredit higher education institutions both public and private; to design and recommend an institutional quality assurance system for higher education.

NCHE (2014) affirms that in order to achieve a reputation for Malawi as one of the top providers of quality higher education in Africa in a variety of disciplines, and to maintain excellence, it is essential that the NCHE ensure institutionalization of quality control measures through all institutions of higher education, whether public or private, and the rationalization of the provision of programmes at all levels: certificates, diploma, undergraduate degree and postgraduate degree.

These measures will serve to guarantee to all stakeholders that the qualifications awarded meet international standards.

The standards and guidelines for quality assurance in Malawi's Higher Education Institutions has been prepared by NCHE. NCHE (2014) mentions that in developing these guidelines, a number of documents from other institutions across the world were taken into account, with the most influential being Standards and Guidelines for Quality Assurance for Accreditation of Higher Education Institutions in Malawi, in order to ensure that institutions seeking accreditation are fully aware of the requirements for compliance on all aspects of quality assurance.

Many quality assurance professionals say that there is increasing interest in higher education quality and standards, reflecting both the rapid growth of higher education and its cost to the public and private purse. This means that if Malawi is to achieve its aspiration to be dynamic and knowledge-based economy, then its higher education sector will need to demonstrate that it takes seriously the quality of its programmes and awards and is willing to put in place the means of as- suring and demonstrating that quality.

It goes without saying that quality assurance in higher education has become a key component in the delivery of education in almost all countries in the world since this effects standards.

Most literature shows that institutions of higher education globally are now aiming at internationalization of their programmes, which can be done if the standards are acceptable to all stakeholders. Malawi is no exception to the quest for quality assurance and this need is demonstrated by the pub- lic debate on the quality of education.

As stated earlier according to NCHE (2014) the NCHE in Malawi was established to act as the body for scrutinizing national qualifications, registering institutions and approving academic programmes for higher education in Malawi. The purpose of the guidelines crafted by NCHE is to assist providers of higher education in designing quality assurance procedures for academic purposes and the guidelines as advocated by NCHE are underpinned by the following principles: programmes should address the interests of students, employers and the society more generally through good quality higher education; institutional autonomy is critically important, tempered by a recognition that this brings with it heavy responsibilities; external quality assurance has to be fit for purposes and to place only an appropriate and necessary burden on institutions for the achievement of their objectives (NCHE 2014)

Internal Quality Assurance Assessment

If we agree upon a shared concept of quality and the criteria and standards to measure our quality, we can ask ourselves: what is the best way to discover our quality? An important tool in the field of quality assurance is a criteria self-assessment, also called, self-evaluation or SWOT- analysis. In this handbook the words are used interchangeably.

A critical assessment is important because we are sometimes too eager to accept that everything is good. "I have been teaching this way for years and my course has never caused problems.

My students have always been content and employers have never complained about the graduates." This may be true in general. In an educational organization, which is a professional organization, the players should always aim to produce quality, Introducing a quality assurance system does not mean that the existing quality is not good enough. The demand for self-evaluation is not inspired by lack of quality. What it means is that quality has to be exempted in a structural manner within a well defined framework.

The Self Assessment for Discovering Quality

In many cases a self-assessment serves as a preparation for a site visit by external experts such as NCHE quality assurance assessment team. The self-assessment report (SAR) provides the external experts with basic information. However, self-assessment has specific value for the University itself too. It provides an opportunity for discovering quality. Therefore, the following questions are important:

1. Why do we do what we are doing? Do we indeed do the right things?
2. Do we do the right things in the right way?
3. Do we have thorough command of the process to actually realize what we want?
4. Do we really achieve what we want to?

An effective self-assessment is time-consuming. It requires effort by staff and students. Often, it will require an investment of time that has to be taken away from other activities. However, the results and the profits of a good self-assessment are high.

Principles of Effective Self-assessment

In organizing an effective self-assessment, one has to take account some basic principles:

Primarily, a self-assessment should never be felt as threatening. A self-assessment should not be used to assess an individual, should never be used for punishment or reward and should never be used to blame someone.

A self-assessment aims at improvement and enhancement of the quality

It is necessary to create a broad basis for the self-assessment and to sensitize staff and students. The whole institution has to prepare itself for it Looking at quality in than testing the performance. It also means organizational development and shaping the University. Everybody has to be responsible and involved for real self-assessment

The institution management must fully support the self-assessment. Relevant information is needed for an effective policy and good management. The self-assessment serves to acquire structural insight in performance of the University carrying out a critical self-assessment process. It would be good to designate someone specifically with the self-evaluation project.

The coordination has to meet some requirements

In order to obtain the required information it is important that the coordinator has good entry rapport at all levels of the University. Therefore it is very important that the coordinator has good contacts within the University, with central management as well as with the faculties and the staff members.

The coordinator must have the authority to make appointments

It is desirable to constitute a substantive team of staff in-charge of the assessment It is important that the team is structured in such a way that the involvement of all sections is assured. The working group is in charge of the self-assessment, gathering data, analyzing materials and drawing conclusions. It is assumed that self-assessment is an analysis supported by the whole acquainted with contents of the self-assessment report and should recognize it as a document of the University. Not everyone has to agree with all the points in the self-assessment report. There may be disagreement as to what are seen as weakness and strengths and what is to be considered as the causes of the weaknesses. Should there be very big differences of opinion between certain groups then the SAR should report on it.

The Organization of the Self-assessment

The University determines how self-assessment is carried out. However, it is good to make use of experiences gained elsewhere. On the basis of experiences with self-assessment in other Universities some suggestions may be made that can facilitate the process.

Self assessment should not be the work of single person

Make a group reasonable for the self-assessment:
   This group should consist some three to five people chaired by the coordinator appointed by the faculty. Students should be involved in the assessment. A clear time table should be set up assuming a total amount of time available of about five to six months between the moment of the for- mal announcement and the actual visit.
   The topics or areas that have to be considered in the self-evaluation should be distributed among the committee members and each member made responsible for collecting information and for analyzing and evaluating the data from the self assessment. The draft results should be discussed on the largest scale possible. It is not necessary to have consensus concerning the report; it is however, necessary for as many people as possible to be aware of its contents

Table 1.1: The Process of Organizing Self Assessment

DATE

Eight months before the planned end of the self-assessment

The following 6 months

Four Months after the start

About 5 Months after the start

Six Months after the start

Eight months after the start

Source: Author (2015)

ACTIVITY

Appoint the leader of the assessment process, compose the assessment team, including students

Divide the cells to be dealt with

Each person responsible for collecting information and data collects that information

Write draft information on the cells

Discussion on the drafts in the group

Second draft

Discussion of the second draft with all faculty staff and students during an opening hearing

Edit the comments of the hearing for the final draft

External assessment

Make the text in red in 2 column on the left would be the date and activity on the right

The self-assessment must be finalized with a self-assessment report (SAR). There are several conditions to be set for SAR. The SAR contains a clear description of the state-of-the-art and a critical analysis of the current situation to see if one is satisfied with it or not. Furthermore, it states clearly what actions will be taken to solve the problems.

The manner in which self-assessments are carried out can vary; also the levels of who is to be involved in the discussion of the report will differ from University to University. Nevertheless the responsibility for the self-assessment lies with the assessment team because the self-assessment is the input of the external assessment it is important for the SAR to follow the specific format as given in the handbook. The SAR is the starting point for the discussions between the external experts and the faculty. This implies that everyone who will be involved in the decision needs to be aware of the contents of the self-evaluation.

The quantitative data requires special attention. The manner in which data are presented is important for the right interpretation. There is a clear need for harmonization of data such as student numbers, appointment of teaching staff, staff/student ratios, success rates, etc

Standards and Criteria to be applied

There are 18 aspects to be considered for the programme assessment: These include;

- ☐ Requirements of Stakeholders
- ☐ Goals and Objectives; expected outcomes

- ☐ Program Content
- ☐ Program Specification or description
- ☐ Program Organization
- ☐ Didactic Concept / Teaching / Learning Strategy
- ☐ Student Assessment
- ☐ Quality of Academic Staff
- ☐ Quality of Support Staff
- ☐ Student Profile
- ☐ Student Advice / Support
- ☐ Facilities and Infrastructure
- ☐ Student Evaluation
- ☐ Curriculum Design and Evaluation
- ☐ Staff Development Activities
- ☐ Bench Marking
- ☐ Achievements / Graduates
- ☐ Satisfaction of Stakeholders

An analysis model for teaching and learning

An institution for Higher Education generally has three core activities: teaching, learning, research and community outreach. Of course the last two activities are important too. However in the handbook the emphasis is on the quality of educational task. To find out the quality of education, the instrument of self-assessment at program level is used. The object of the assessment is the program.

A program is defined as a coherent set of courses leading to certain degree (bachelor or masters). We may call the program also a curriculum.

As mentioned earlier quality is a concept with many aspects. These are many factors influencing quality. With regard to Teaching and Learning, the following dimensions can be distinguished:

- ☐ Quality of the input
- ☐ Quality of the process
- ☐ Quality of the output

Therefore in order to map the quality in a self-assessment we need a clear model to guard against looking at some aspects and ignoring others.

The basic rules to apply in the self-assessments are: All aspects need to be discussed. It is not possible to make a selection. For each cell the following steps are to be taken:

- ☐ Description
- ☐ Analysis
- ☐ Formulation of Strengths and Weaknesses
- ☐ Evidence of Meeting the Criteria
- ☐ Action Plan for Improvement
- ☐ When it is the first time do not worry too much about white spots. Include them in the action plan

External Quality Assurance Assessment

Before an external expert team from National Council of Higher Education starts the site visit to the University, the responsible internal quality assurance team should have carried out an internal self assessment of the programs and facilities including the infrastructure to be assessed. A self- assessment is an important instrument in the hands of a university when it comes to seeing what quality it offers. A good self-assessment, done very carefully, critically and analytically offers the faculty/department a good view on the state-of-the-art and on the quality itself. However, a self- assessment is not enough. We all have blind spots and take things for granted. Therefore, an outside's view of the performance is needed. An external assessment by an expert team is an additional instrument, to learn more about the quality.

An external assessment is important because it gives authority to the findings of the self assessment. If we state that our faculty is performing badly, everybody will believe us. If we say that we are performing excellently, nobody will believe us, because the outside world say: "that is their own assessment, how can we trust it?" External assessment also delivers confidence to stakeholders; provides evidence of quality to the public; and shows that the standards agreed upon by the competent authorities are being implemented. At the same time, it provides mechanisms for continuous quality improvement in the sustainability and development of the program and buffers against pressures to lower quality standards.

External quality assessment contributes to the recognition and acceptance of programs that have demonstrated their competence and quality according to standard set by the field or profession leading towards harmonisation of higher education in the region. Graduates of these programs are likewise recognised for their competent training and employability. External assessment also provides opportunities for accessing funding for research and development.

Preparing for the assessment

An external assessment require good preparation. The role of experts is not an easy one. The expert team has to combine various functions. The team will:

- ☐ Check thew outcomes of the self-assessment
- ☐ Reflect on the self- Engage in dialogue and discussion with staff and student
- ☐ Act as an auditor

An external expert team is required to combine two missions:

- ☐ The team members should listen to the faculty and act as colleagues, using their expertise and experience to offer advice and recommendations.
- ☐ At the same time, the team has to write a report that might be made public or remain confidential. However, the team will give its independent verdict on the quality in that report. In one way the team of experts has to act collegially and in the other way it has to remain independent. It will not always be easy to combine the divergent.

Preparation of the external assessment team

In general, the task of the expert team can be described as follows:

- ☐ To form an opinion about the standard of the program and the quality of the educational process, including the organisation of education and the standard of the graduates on the basis of information supplied by the faculty and by means of discussions held on site. In assessing quality, the team will look at the requirements and expectations of the student, the faculty/discipline and society, and, in particular, prospective employers.

☐ To make suggestions on quality improvement. An assessment team trying to fulfil its task will encounter a lot of problems, because the generally formulated task means that the team will tend to form opinions about everything.

The assessment

After the preparatory meeting, the expert team will come together for the site visit. If the preparatory meeting was held on the day before the site visit, the team will start directly with the site visit.

What is the external assessment team looking for?

The expert team assesses the quality of the program. The team will already have discussed several aspects during the preliminary meeting. The SAR will already have provided detailed information. During the site visit, the team will be looking for evidence with the intentions in mind:

☐ Assessing quality of academic and support staff, students, facilities and infrastructure
☐ Are the objectives /the expected learning outcomes clearly formulated?
☐ How are these translated into the curriculum?
☐ Do the exams reflect the content o the program and courses?
☐ Are graduates going to acquire the expected knowledge, skills and attitudes

The team is on a fact-finding mission. Of course, the SAR is the basic source of information and should provide the basic information. But other sources should also be used:

☐ The interviews
☐ The list of the literature used
☐ Assessment and examination papers
☐ Course descriptions and readers

Table 1.2: checklist on the quality of a program

	Score						
	1	2	3	4	5	6	7
1. Requirements of stakeholders. The faculty/ department has a clear idea							
about the relevant needs and requirements of the government							
about the relevant needs and requirement of the labour market							
about the relevant needs and requirement of the students/parents about the relevant needs and requirement of the academic world							
about the relevant needs and requirement of the society							
Overall opinion							
2. expected learning outcomes (objectives)							
the program has clearly formulated learning outcomes							
the program promotes learning to learn and life-long learning							
the expected learning outcomes cover generic skills and knowledge as well as specific skills and knowledge							
the expected learning outcomes clearly reflect the requirements of the stakeholders							
Overall opinion							
3. program specification							
the university uses program specification/program description							
the program specification shows the expected learning outcomes							
the program specification is informative for the stakeholders							
Overall opinion							
4. Program content							
The program content shows a good balance between general and specific skills and knowledge							

the program reflects the vision and mission of the university						
The expected learning outcomes have been adequately translated into the program						
the contribution made by each course to achieve the learning outcomes is clear						

Source: Author (2015

Qualifications Framework and Recognition of Qualifications

This guidance is about the implementation of the framework for higher education qualifications in Malawi. It applies to degrees, diplomas, certificates and other academic awards granted by a higher education provider1 in the exercise of its degree awarding powers. Qualifications Frame- work and Recognition of Qualifications (QFRQ) is an important reference point for providers of higher education. The QFRQ, and associated guidance for implementation, has been written to assist higher education providers to maintain academic standards; to inform national comparability of academic standards, especially in the Malawi context; to ensure international competitiveness; and to facilitate student and graduate mobility. Higher education providers may find it useful to refer to the QFRQ in their discussions with the main stakeholders in higher education (prospective students, parents, schools, employers and Government) about the outcomes and attributes that each qualification represents.

Qualification descriptors set out the generic outcomes and attributes expected for the award of individual qualifications. The qualification descriptors contained in the QFRQ exemplify the outcomes and attributes expected of learning that results in the award of higher education qualifications. These outcomes represent the integration of various learning experiences resulting from designated and coherent programmes of study.

The QFRQ is also used as a reference point in institutional audit/ review and other forms of external review. Audit and review teams will examine the means which higher education providers use to ensure that their awards and qualifications are of an academic standard at least consistent with those referred to in the QFRQ, and that higher education providers are, where relevant, exercising their powers as degree awarding bodies in a proper manner. In particular, audit and review teams will wish to look at how higher education providers check the alignment between the academic standards of their awards and the levels referred to in the QFRQ. In this regard, the QFRQ should be regarded as a framework, not as a straitjacket.

The purpose of the QFRQ

Public confidence in academic standards requires public understanding of the achievements represented by higher education qualifications. The main purposes of the QFRQ to: provide important points of reference for setting and assessing academic standards to higher education providers and their external examiners assist in the identification of potential progression routes, particularly in the context of lifelong learning; promote a shared and common understanding of the expectations associated with typical qualifications by facilitating a consistent use of qualifications titles across the higher education sector in Malawi.

As a result, the QFRQ should enable higher education providers to communicate to employers; schools; parents; prospective students; professional, statutory and regulatory bodies (PSRBs); and other stakeholders the achievements and attributes represented by the typical higher education qualification titles. The reviewers use the QFRQ as a reference point when auditing or reviewing the establishment and management of academic standards by higher education providers. In particular, auditors and reviewers look at how institutions align the academic standards of their awards with the levels referred to in the QFRQ. They also ascertain whether institutions have means of ensuring that awards and qualifications are of an academic standard at least consistent with the standards referred to in the QFRQ. Similarly, the QFRQ is an important tool for PSRBs in defining and using qualifications in the context of their accreditation processes.

The number of levels in the QFRQ

The levels of the QFRQ, with examples of typical qualifications at each level, are represented in Table 1.3 below.

Typical Higher Education Qualifications	QFRQ
Doctoral of Philosophy Degree (Ph.D)	65
Master's Degree	43
Bachelor's Degree	2
University Diploma	
University Certificate	

Source: Author (2015)

Typically, programmes leading to higher education qualifications, particularly those taken over a number of years, include learning that is progressively more challenging. For the award of a higher education qualification at a particular level, the outcomes of this learning must reflect, in an holistic way, the qualification descriptor for that level.

Positioning qualifications within the QFRQ

When positioning higher education qualifications within the QFRQ, higher education providers will wish to assure the public that the achievements represented by qualifications are appropriate and represented consistently. Higher education providers are responsible for demonstrating that each of their qualifications is allocated to the appropriate level of the QFRQ. In considering the appropriate level for a qualification, higher education providers consider: the relationship between the intended outcomes of the programme and the expectations set out in the qualification descriptors; whether there is a sufficient volume of assessed study that will demonstrate that the learning outcomes have been achieved; whether the design of the curriculum and assessments is such that all students following the programme have the opportunity to achieve and demonstrate the intended outcomes.

When designing and approving programmes, higher education providers will wish to ensure that a coherent learning experience is delivered and that due consideration is given to the precept and explanatory text relating to programme design in the Code of practice for the assurance of academic quality and standards in higher education. In addition, higher education providers will wish to take account of the regulatory and other requirements of the PSRBs which accredit specific professional programmes.

Qualification Descriptor

The qualifications are differentiated by the volume of learning and this in turn leads to variation in the range of intended learning outcomes. Some qualifications (for instance Foundation Degrees) have been specifically designed to facilitate progression to subsequent levels. This section provides further information about the qualification descriptor for each level of the framework and gives examples of qualifications that meet each descriptor in full, and where the qualification descriptor can be used as a reference point for other qualifications at the same level.

Descriptors exemplify the nature and characteristics of the main qualification at each level, and comparison demonstrates the nature and characteristics of change between qualifications at different levels. They provide clear points of reference at each level and describe outcomes that cover the great majority of existing qualifications. However, the QFRQ has the flexibility to accommodate diversity and innovation, and to accommodate new qualifications as the need for them arises.

Qualification descriptors are in two parts. The first part is a statement of outcomes, achievement of which is assessed and which a student should be able to demonstrate for the award of the qualification. This part will be of particular relevance to higher education providers in designing, approving and reviewing academic programmes. They will need to be satisfied that, for any programme, the curriculum and assessments provide all students with the opportunity to achieve, and to demonstrate achievement of, the intended outcomes.

The second part is a statement of the wider abilities that the typical student could be expected to have developed. It will be of assistance to higher education providers during discussions with employers, and others with an interest in the general capabilities of holders of the qualification. Each descriptor sets out the outcomes for the typical qualification at each level - for levels 5 and 6 this is usually a degree. 'Naming qualifications', provides further guidance on the naming of qualifications and specifically the use of the title 'degree' for both undergraduate and postgraduate awards at all levels.

At most levels there may be more than one type of qualification which can be achieved. Short programmes are often offered as continuing professional development opportunities. The qualification descriptors provide points of reference that will help institutions determine at which level of the QFRQ any qualifications resulting from such programmes should be placed. The guidance on naming qualifications may be used to determine an appropriate title. A range of qualifications are encompassed by each level of the QFRQ. Each level is deliberately broad to provide flexibility and space for the development of new qualifications, for example, occupationally related awards.

Descriptor for a higher education qualification at level 2: Certificate of Higher Education

The descriptor provided for this level of the QFRQ is for any Certificate of Higher Education which should meet the descriptor in full. This qualification descriptor can also be used as a reference point for other level 2 qualifications. Certificates of Higher Education are awarded to students who have demonstrated:

Knowledge of the underlying concepts and principles associated with their area(s) of study, and an ability to evaluate and interpret these within the context of that area of study an ability to present, evaluate and interpret qualitative and quantitative data, in order to develop lines of argument and make sound judgements in accordance with basic theories and concepts of their subject (s) of study.

Typically, holders of the qualification will be able to: evaluate the appropriateness of different approaches to solving problems related to their area(s) of study and/or work; communicate the results of their study/work accurately and reliably, and with structured and coherent arguments and undertake further training and develop new skills within a structured and managed environment. And holders will have: the qualities and transferable skills necessary for employment requiring the exercise of some personal responsibility.

Holders of a Certificate of Higher Education will have a sound knowledge of the basic concepts of a subject, and will have learned how to take different approaches to solving problems. They will be able to communicate accurately and will have the qualities needed for employment requiring the exercise of some personal responsibility. The Certificate of Higher Education may be a first step towards obtaining higher level qualifications.

Descriptor for a higher education qualification at level 4: Bachelor's Degree

The descriptor provided for this level of the QFRQ is for any Bachelor's Degree which should meet the descriptor in full. This qualification descriptor can also be used as a reference point for other level 4 qualifications, including University Diplomas, etc.

Bachelor's Degree are awarded to students who have demonstrated:

knowledge and critical understanding of the well-established principles of their area(s) of study, and of the way in which those principles have developed ability to apply underlying concepts and principles outside the context in which they were first studied, including, where appropriate, the application of those principles in an employment context knowledge of the main methods of enquiry in the subject(s) relevant to the named award, and ability to evaluate critically the appropriateness of different approaches to solving problems in the field of study an understanding of the limits of their knowledge, and how this influences anal- yses and interpretations based on that knowledge.

Typically, holders of the qualification will be able to: use a range of established techniques to initiate and undertake critical analysis of information, and to propose solutions to problems arising from that analysis; effectively communicate information, arguments and analysis in a variety of forms to specialist and non-specialist audiences, and deploy key techniques of the discipline effectively, undertake further training, develop existing skills and acquire new competences that will enable them to assume significant responsibility within organisations.

And holders will have: the qualities and transferable skills necessary for employment requiring the exercise of personal responsibility and decision-making. The Bachelor's Degree is an example of a qualification that meets, in full, the expectations of the qualification descriptor. Holders of qualifications at this level will have developed a sound understanding of the principles in their field of study, and will have learned to apply those principles more widely. Through this, they will have learned to evaluate the appropriateness of different approaches to solving problems. Holders of qualifications at this level will have the qualities necessary for employment in situations requir- ing the exercise of personal responsibility and decision-making. On the other hand Bachelor's degrees with honours are awarded to students who have demonstrated: a systematic understanding of key aspects of their field of study, including acquisition of coherent and detailed knowledge, at least some of which is at, or informed by, the forefront of defined aspects of a discipline; an ability to deploy accurately established techniques of analysis and enquiry within a discipline; conceptual understanding that enables the student:

To devise and sustain arguments, and/or to solve problems, using ideas and techniques, some of which are at the forefront of a discipline.

To describe and comment upon particular aspects of current research, or equivalent advanced scholarship, in the discipline an appreciation of the uncertainty, ambiguity and limits of knowledge the ability to manage their own learning, and to make use of scholarly reviews and primary sources (for example, refereed research articles and/or original materials appropriate to the discipline).

Typically, holders of the qualification will be able to: apply the methods and techniques that they have learned to review, consolidate, extend and apply their knowledge and understanding, and to initiate and carry out projects; critically evaluate arguments, assumptions, abstract concepts and data (that may be incomplete), to make judgements, and to frame appropriate questions to achieve a solution - or identify a range of solutions - to a problem; communicate information, ideas, problems and solutions to both specialist and non-specialist audiences. And holders will have: the qualities and transferable skills necessary for employment requiring: the exercise of initiative and personal responsibility decision-making in complex and unpredictable contexts the learning ability needed to undertake appropriate further training of a professional or equivalent nature.

Holders of a bachelor's degree with honours will have developed an understanding of a complex body of knowledge, some of it at the current boundaries of an academic discipline. Through this, the holder will have developed analytical techniques and problem-solving skills that can be applied in many types of employment. The holder of such a qualification will be able to evaluate evidence, arguments and assumptions, to reach sound judgements and to communicate them effectively. Holders of a bachelor's degree with honours should have the qualities needed for employment in situations requiring the exercise of personal responsibility, and decision-making in complex and unpredictable circumstances.

Descriptor for a higher education qualification at level 5: Master's Degree

The descriptor provided for this level of the framework is for any master's degree which should meet the descriptor in full. This qualification descriptor can also be used as a reference point for other level qualifications, including postgraduate certificates and postgraduate diplomas.

Master's degrees are awarded to students who have demonstrated:

> systematic understanding of knowledge, and a critical awareness of current problems and/or new insights, much of which is at, or informed by, the forefront of their academic discipline, field of study or area of professional practice a comprehensive understanding of techniques applicable to their own research or advanced scholarship originality in the application of knowledge, together with a practical understanding of how established techniques of research and enquiry are used to create and interpret knowledge in the discipline conceptual understanding that enables the student: to evaluate critically current research and advanced scholarship in the discipline; to evaluate methodologies and develop critiques of them and, where appropriate, to propose new hypotheses.

Typically, holders of the qualification will be able to: deal with complex issues both system- atically and creatively, make sound judgements in the absence of complete data, and communicate their conclusions clearly to specialist and non-specialist audiences, demonstrate self-direction and originality in tackling and solving problems, and act autonomously in planning and implementing tasks at a professional or equivalent level, continue to advance their knowledge and understanding, and to develop new skills to a high level. And holders will have: the qualities and transferable skills necessary for employment requiring: the exercise of initiative and personal responsibility, decision-making in complex and unpredictable situations the independent learning ability required for continuing professional development.

Much of the study undertaken for master's degrees will have been at, or informed by, the forefront of an academic or professional discipline. Students will have shown originality in the application of knowledge, and they will understand how the boundaries of knowledge are advanced through research. They will be able to deal with complex issues both systematically and creatively, and they will show originality in tackling and solving problems. They will have the qualities needed for employment in circumstances requiring sound judgement, personal responsibility and initiative in complex and unpredictable professional environments.

Master's degrees are awarded after completion of taught courses, programmes of research or a mixture of both. Master's degrees are often distinguished from other qualifications at this level (for example, advanced short courses, which often form parts of continuing professional development programmes and lead to postgraduate certificates and/or postgraduate diplomas) by an increased intensity, complexity and density of study. Master's degrees - in comparison to postgraduate certificates and postgraduate diplomas - typically include planned intellectual progression that often includes a synoptic/research or scholarly activity.

Doctoral degrees are awarded to students who have demonstrated:

The creation and interpretation of new knowledge, through original research or other advanced scholarship, of a quality to satisfy peer review, extend the forefront of the discipline, and merit publicationa systematic acquisition and understanding of a substantial body of knowledge which is at the forefront of an academic discipline or area of professional practice the general ability to conceptualise, design and implement a project for the generation of new knowledge, applications or understanding at the forefront of the discipline, and to adjust the project design in the light of unforeseen problems a detailed understanding of applicable techniques for research and advanced academic enquiry.

Typically, holders of the qualification will be able to: make informed judgements on complex issues in specialist fields, often in the absence of complete data, and be able to communicate their ideas and conclusions clearly and effectively to specialist and non-specialist audiences; continue to undertake pure and/or applied research and development at an advanced level, contributing substantially to the development of new techniques, ideas or approaches. And holders will have: the qualities and transferable skills necessary for employment requiring the exercise of personal responsibility and largely autonomous initiative in complex and unpredictable situations, in professional or equivalent environments.

Doctoral degrees are awarded for the creation and interpretation, construction and/or exposition of knowledge which extends the forefront of a discipline, usually through original research. Holders of doctoral degrees will be able to conceptualise, design and implement projects for the generation of significant new knowledge and/or understanding. Holders of doctoral degrees will have the qualities needed for employment that require both the ability to make informed judgements on complex issues in specialist fields and an innovative approach to tackling and solving problems.

The titles PhD are commonly used for doctoral degrees awarded on the basis of original research. Achievement of outcomes consistent with the qualification descriptor for the doctoral degree normally requires study equivalent to three full-time calendar years.

Note: Honorary doctoral degrees are not academic qualifications.

The relationship between qualification descriptors and other points of reference for academic standards

Qualification descriptors are linked to other parts of the Academic Infrastructure in the following ways:

Qualification descriptors are generic statements of the intended outcomes of study. Many academic programmes aim to develop general and specific skills. These are not explicitly addressed in the qualification descriptors as many skills, and the extent to which they need to be developed, are discipline or profession specific. As such, they are addressed more appropriately in subject benchmark statements and individual programme specifications.

More detailed statements on the expected outcomes in particular subjects can be found in subject benchmark statements. These have been produced for typical and threshold standards in bachelor's degrees with honours, and have been produced for other levels where there is significant taught provision in a subject (for example, MEng). A single qualifications benchmark statement has also been produced to provide a reference point for the Foundation Degree qualification.

In areas where there is no benchmark statement, or where more than one such statement may be relevant, the statements of generic outcomes contained in the qualification descriptors provide a particularly important point of reference. Specific statements about the intended outcomes of an individual programme are provided by institutions in programme specifications. These define the specific outcomes of learning for a qualification in a particular subject area offered by that institution.

For any qualification, study leading directly to the qualification will normally build on learning from earlier stages of a programme of study, or from other assessed prior learning. Providers of higher education programmes need to be able to demonstrate how the design of curricula facilitates academic and intellectual progression. However, it is for providers to decide how this is best demonstrated, whether by a credit structure or otherwise.

The FQRQ - implementation issues and guidance

The following guidance identifies key matters that a higher education provider should be able to demonstrate it is addressing effectively through its own quality assurance mechanisms. The accompanying explanatory text is neither prescriptive nor exhaustive, but for many higher education providers it will constitute appropriate good practice.

Naming qualifications

The title of any qualification accurately reflects the level of achievements, represents appropriately the nature and field(s) of study undertaken and is not misleading. Public understanding of the achievements represented by higher education qualifications requires a transparent use of qualification titles. The following guidance is designed to assist institutions in achieving clarity and consistency in the ways in which qualification titles convey information about the level, nature and subjects of study.

To ensure that the name given to any qualification within the FQR appropriately represents its level, and to promote public understanding of the achievements represented by higher education qualifications, clarity in the use of qualification titles is required. The following guidance is designed to assist higher education providers in achieving clarity and consistency in the ways in which qualification titles convey accurately information about the level of the qualification: the titles 'honours' (for example, bachelor's degree with honours), 'master' (for example, Master of Arts) and 'doctor' (for example, Doctor of Philosophy) should be used only for qualifications that meet, in full, the expectations of the qualification descriptors at level 4, level 5 and level 6 respectively; titles with the stem 'postgraduate' (for example, postgraduate diploma) should be restricted to qualifications where the learning outcomes of the programme of study match relevant parts of the descriptor for a qualification at level 6 or above; titles with the stem 'graduate' (for example, graduate diploma) should be used for qualifications from programmes of study that typically require graduate entry, or its equivalent, and have learning outcomes that match relevant parts of the descriptor for a qualification at level 4.

Awarding qualifications

Qualifications are awarded to mark the achievement of positively defined outcomes, not as compensation for failure at a higher level, or by default. Failure at a higher level does not mean that a lower qualification cannot be awarded. However, where a student does not demonstrate the outcomes set out in a qualification descriptor, a lower qualification should only be awarded if the student has demonstrated the outcomes required for that qualification. Higher education providers ensure that: the outcomes required for each of their qualifications are specified clearly achievement of those outcomes is demonstrated before a qualification is awarded assessment procedures that permit compensation or condonation are not applied in a way that might allow a qualification to be awarded without achievement of the full outcomes being demonstrated.

Standards and Guidelines for Internal Quality Assurance

NCHE (2014) advocates that institutions should have a policy and associated procedures for the assurance of the quality and standards of their programmes and awards. They should also commit themselves explicitly to the development of culture which recognizes the importance of quality and quality assurance, in their work. To achieve this, institutions are expected to develop and implement a strategy for the continuous enhancement of quality. The policy, strategy and procedures should have formal status and be publically available. The role of students and stakeholders should also be included.

NCHE (2014) points out that the guidelines on policy and procedures provide a framework within which higher education institutions can develop and monitor the effectiveness of their quality assurance systems. They also help to provide public confidence in institutional autonomy. Policies contain the statements of intentions and the principal means by which will be achieved. Procedural guidance can give more detailed information about the ways in which the policy is implemented and provides a useful reference point for those who need to know about the practical aspects of carrying out the procedures. According to NCHE (2014) the policy statement is expected to include: the relationship between teaching and research and research in institution; the institution's strategy for quality and standards; the organization of the quality assurance system; the responsibilities of departments, schools, faculties and other organizational units and individuals for the assurance of quality; the involvement of students in quality assurance, e.g. through course assessments and the ways in which the policy is implemented, monitored and revised, e.g. through trace studies, periodic reviews, feedback from stakeholders among others.

It goes without saying that the realisation of the NCHE quality assurance procedures depends crucially on a commitment at all levels of an institution to ensuring that its programmes have clear and explicit intended outcomes; that its staff are ready, willing and able to provide teaching and learner support that will help its students achieve those outcomes; and there is full, timely and tangible recognition of the contribution to work by those of its staff who demonstrate particular excellence, expertise and dedication. All higher education institutions should aspire to improve and enhance the education they offer their students.

Policy for quality assurance

Standard: Institutions should have a policy for quality assurance that is made public and forms part of their strategic management. Internal stakeholders should develop and implement this policy through appropriate structures and processes, while involving external stakeholders.

Guidelines: Policies and processes are the main pillars of a coherent institutional quality assurance system that forms a cycle for continuous improvement and contributes to the accountability of the institution. It supports the development of quality culture in which all internal stakeholders assume responsibility for quality and engage in quality assurance at all levels of the institution. In order to facilitate this, the policy has a formal status and is publicly available.

Quality assurance policies are most effective when they reflect the relationship between research and learning & teaching and take account of both the national context in which the institution operates, the institutional context and its strategic approach. Such a policy supports the organisation of the quality assurance system; departments, schools, faculties and other organisational units as well as those of institutional leadership, individual staff members and students to take on their responsibilities in quality assurance; academic integrity and freedom and is vigilant against academic fraud; guarding against intolerance of any kind or discrimination against the students or staff; and the involvement of external stakeholders in quality assurance.

The policy translates into practice through a variety of internal quality assurance processes that allow participation across the institution. How the policy is implemented, monitored and revised is the institution's decision. The quality assurance policy also covers any elements of an institution's activities that are subcontracted to or carried out by other parties.

Design and approval of programmes

Standard: Institutions should have processes for the design and approval of their programmes. The programmes should be designed so that they meet the objectives set for them, including the intended learning outcomes. The qualification resulting from a programme should be clearly specified and communicated, and refer to the correct level of the national qualifications framework for higher education and, consequently, to the Framework for Qualifications of the NCHE in Malawi.

Guidelines: Study programmes are at the core of the higher education institutions' teaching mission. They provide students with both academic knowledge and skills including those that are transferable, which may influence their personal development and may be applied in their future careers.

Programmes are designed with overall programme objectives that are in line with the institutional strategy and have explicit intended learning outcomes; are designed by involving students and other stakeholders in the work; benefit from external expertise and reference points; reflect the five purposes of NCHE; are designed so that they enable smooth student progression; define the expected student workload include well-structured placement opportunities where appropriate and are subject to a formal institutional approval process.

Student-centred learning, teaching and assessment

Standard: Institutions should ensure that the programmes are delivered in a way that encourages students to take an active role in creating the learning process, and that the assessment of students reflects this approach.

Guidelines: Student-centred learning and teaching plays an important role in stimulating students' motivation, self-reflection and engagement in the learning process. This means careful consideration of the design and delivery of study programmes and the assessment of outcomes. The implementation of student-centred learning and teaching: respects and attends to the diversity of students and their needs, enabling flexible learning paths; considers and uses different modes of delivery, where appropriate; flexibly uses a variety of pedagogical methods; regularly evaluates and adjusts the modes of delivery and pedagogical methods; encourages a sense of autonomy in the learner, while ensuring adequate guidance and support from the teacher; promotes mutual respect within the learner-teacher relationship; has appropriate procedures for dealing with students' complaints.

Considering the importance of assessment for the students' progression and their future careers, quality assurance processes for assessment take into account the following: Placements include traineeships, internships and other periods of the programme that are not spent in the institution but that allow the student to gain experience in an area related to their studies; Assessors are familiar with existing testing and examination methods and receive support in developing their own skills in this field; Ensure that the criteria for and method of assessment as well as criteria for marking are published in advance; The assessment allows students to demonstrate the extent to which the intended learning outcomes have been achieved. Students are given feedback, which, if necessary, is linked to advice on the learning process; Where possible, assessment is carried out by more than one examiner; The regulations for assessment take into account mitigating circumstances; Assessment is consistent, fairly applied to all students and carried out in accordance with the stated procedures; and a formal procedure for student appeals is in place.

Student admission, progression, recognition and certification

Standard: Institutions should consistently apply pre-defined and published regulations covering all phases of the student "life cycle", e.g. student admission, progression, recognition and certification.

Guidelines: Providing conditions and support that are necessary for students to make progress in their academic career is in the best interest of the individual students, programmes, institutions and systems. It is vital to have fit-for-purpose admission, recognition and completion procedures, particularly when students are mobile within and across higher education systems.

It is important that access policies, admission processes and criteria are implemented consistently and in a transparent manner. Induction to the institution and the programme is provided. Institutions need to put in place both processes and tools to collect, monitor and act on information on student progression.

Fair recognition of higher education qualifications, periods of study and prior learning, including the recognition of non-formal and informal learning, are essential components for ensuring the students' progress in their studies, while promoting mobility. Appropriate recognition procedures rely on institutional practice for recognition being in line with the principles of the Lisbon Recognition Convention; cooperation with other institutions, quality assurance agencies and the NCHE with a view to ensuring coherent recognition across the country.

Graduation represents the culmination of the students' period of study. Students need to receive documentation explaining the qualification gained, including achieved learning outcomes and the context, level, content and status of the studies that were pursued and successfully completed.

Teaching staff

Standard: Institutions should assure themselves of the competence of their teachers. They should apply fair and transparent processes for the recruitment and development of the staff.

Guidelines: The teacher's role is essential in creating a high quality student experience and enabling the acquisition of knowledge, competences and skills. The diversifying student population and stronger focus on learning outcomes require student-centered learning and teaching and the role of the teacher is, therefore, also changing.

Higher education institutions have primary responsibility for the quality of their staff and for providing them with a supportive environment that allows them to carry out their work effectively. Such an environment sets up and follows clear, transparent and fair processes for staff recruitment and conditions of employment that recognise the importance of teaching; offers opportunities for and promotes the professional development of teaching staff; encourages scholarly activity to strengthen the link between education and research; and encourages innovation in teaching methods and the use of new technologies.

Learning resources and student support

Standard: Institutions should have appropriate funding for learning and teaching activities and ensure that adequate and readily accessible learning resources and student support are provided.

Guidelines: For a good higher education experience, institutions provide a range of resources to assist student learning. These vary from physical resources such as libraries, study facili- ties and IT infrastructure to human support in the form of tutors, counsellors and other advisers. The role of support services is of particular importance in facilitating the mobility of students with- in and across higher education systems.

The needs of a diverse student population (such as mature, part-time, employed and international students as well as students with disabilities), and the shift towards student centered learning and flexible modes of learning and teaching, are taken into account when allocating, planning and providing the learning resources and student support.

Support activities and facilities may be organised in a variety of ways depending on the institutional context. However, the internal quality assurance ensures that all resources are fit for purpose, accessible, and that students are informed about the services available to them. In delivering support services the role of support and administrative staff is crucial and therefore they need to be qualified and have opportunities to develop their competences.

Information management

Standard: Institutions should ensure that they collect, analyse and use relevant information for the effective management of their programmes and other activities.

Guidelines: Reliable data is crucial for informed decision-making and for knowing what is working well and what needs attention. Effective processes to collect and analyse information about study programmes and other activities feed into the internal quality assurance system.

The information gathered depends, to some extent, on the type and mission of the institution. The following are of interest: Key performance indicators; Profile of the student population; Student progression, success and drop-out rates; Students' satisfaction with their programmes; Learning resources and student support available; Career paths of graduates. Various methods of collecting information may be used. It is important that students and staff are involved in providing and analysing information and planning follow-up activities.

Public information

Standard: Institutions should publish information about their activities, including programmes, which is clear, accurate, objective, up-to date and readily accessible.

Guidelines: Information on institutions' activities is useful for prospective and current students as well as for graduates, other stakeholders and the public.

Therefore, institutions provide information about their activities, including the programmes they offer and the selection criteria for them, the intended learning outcomes of these programmes, the qualifications they award, the teaching, learning and assessment procedures used the pass rates and the learning opportunities available to their students as well as graduate employment information.

On-going monitoring and periodic review of programmes

Standard: Institutions should monitor and periodically review their programmes to ensure that they achieve the objectives set for them and respond to the needs of students and society. These reviews should lead to continuous improvement of the programme. Any action planned or taken as a result should be communicated to all those concerned.

Guidelines: Regular monitoring, review and revision of study programmes aim to ensure that the provision remains appropriate and to create a supportive and effective learning environment for students. They include the evaluation of: The content of the programme in the light of the latest research in the given discipline thus ensuring that the programme is up to date; The changing needs of society; The students' workload, progression and completion; The effectiveness of procedures for assessment of students; The student expectations, needs and satisfaction in relation to the programme; The learning environment and support services and their fitness for purpose for the programme.

Programmes are reviewed and revised regularly involving students and other stakeholders. The information collected is analysed and the programme is adapted to ensure that it is up-to-date. Revised programme specifications are published.

Cyclical external quality assurance

Standard: Institutions should undergo external quality assurance in line with the ESG on a cyclical basis.

Guidelines: External quality assurance in its various forms can verify the effectiveness of institutions' internal quality assurance, act as a catalyst for improvement and offer the institution new perspectives. It will also provide information to assure the institution and the public of the quality of the institution's activities.

Institutions participate in cyclical external quality assurance that takes account, where relevant, of the requirements of the legislative framework in which they operate. Therefore, depending on the framework, this external quality assurance may take different forms and focus at different organisational levels (such as programme, faculty or institution). Quality assurance is a continuous process that does not end with the external feedback or report or its follow-up process within the institution. Therefore, institutions ensure that the progress made since the last external quality as- surance activity is taken into consideration when preparing for the next one.

Standards and guidelines for External Quality Assurance

Consideration of external quality assurance

Standard: External quality assurance should address the effectiveness of the internal quality assurance processes presented in chapter 10 of this book.

Guidelines: Quality assurance in higher education is based on the institutions' responsibility for the quality of their programmes and other provision; therefore it is important that external quality assurance recognises and supports institutional responsibility for quality assurance. To ensure the link between internal and external quality assurance, external quality assurance includes consideration of the standards presented in chapter 10. These may be addressed differently, depending on the type of external quality assurance.

Designing methodologies fit for purpose

Standard: External quality assurance should be defined and designed specifically to ensure its fitness to achieve the aims and objectives set for it, while taking into account relevant regulations. Stakeholders should be involved in its design and continuous improvement.

Guidelines: In order to ensure effectiveness and objectivity it is vital for external quality assurance to have clear aims agreed by stakeholders.

The aims, objectives and implementation of the processes will bear in mind the level of workload and cost that they will place on institutions; take into account the need to support institutions to improve quality; allow institutions to demonstrate this improvement; result in clear information on the outcomes and the follow-up.

The system for external quality assurance might operate in a more flexible way if institutions are able to demonstrate the effectiveness of their own internal quality assurance.

Implementing processes

Standard: External quality assurance processes should be reliable, useful, pre-defined, implemented consistently and published. They include a self-assessment or equivalent; an external assessment normally including a site visit; a report resulting from the external assessment; and a consistent follow-up.

Guidelines: External quality assurance carried out professionally, consistently and transparently ensures its acceptance and impact.

Depending on the design of the external quality assurance system, the institution provides the basis for the external quality assurance through a self-assessment or by collecting other material including supporting evidence. The written documentation is normally complemented by interviews with stakeholders during a site visit. The findings of the assessment are summarised in a report written by a group of external experts from NCHE.

External quality assurance does not end with the report by the experts. The report provides clear guidance for institutional action. Agencies have a consistent follow-up process for considering the action taken by the institution. The nature of the follow-up will depend on the design of the external quality assurance.

Peer-review experts

Standard: External quality assurance should be carried out by groups of external experts that include (a) student member(s).

Guidelines: At the core of external quality assurance is the wide range of expertise provided by peer experts, who contribute to the work of the agency through input from various perspectives, including those of institutions, academics, students and employers/professional practitioners. In order to ensure the value and consistency of the work of the experts, they are carefully selected; have appropriate skills and are competent to perform their task; are supported by appropriate training and/or briefing. The agency ensures the independence of the experts by implementing a mechanism of no-conflict- of-interest. The involvement of international experts in external quality assurance, for example as members of peer panels, is desirable as it adds a further dimension to the development and implementation of processes.

Criteria for outcomes

Standard: Any outcomes or judgements made as the result of external quality assurance should be based on explicit and published criteria that are applied consistently, irrespective of whether the process leads to a formal decision.

Guidelines:

External quality assurance and in particular its outcomes have a significant impact on institutions and programmes that are evaluated and judged. In the interests of equity and reliability, out- comes of external quality assurance are based on pre- defined and published criteria, which are interpreted consistently and are evidence-based. Depending on the external quality assurance system, outcomes may take different forms, for example, recommendations, judgements or formal decisions.

Reporting

Standard: Full reports by the experts should be published, clear and accessible to the academic community, external partners and other interested individuals. If the agency takes any for- mal decision based on the reports, the decision should be published together with the report.

Guidelines: The report by the experts is the basis for the institution's follow-up action of the external evaluation and it provides information to society regarding the activities of an institution. In order for the report to be used as the basis for action to be taken, it needs to be clear and concise-up action.

The preparation of a summary report may be useful

The factual accuracy of a report is improved if the institution is given the opportunity to point out errors of fact before the report is finalised.

Complaints and appeals

Standard: Complaints and appeals processes should be clearly defined as part of the design of external quality assurance processes and communicated to the institutions.

Guidelines:
In order to safeguard the rights of the institutions and ensure fair decision-making, external quality assurance is operated in an open and accountable way. Nevertheless, there may be misapprehensions or instances of dissatisfaction about the process or formal outcomes.

Institutions need to have access to processes that allow them to raise issues of concern with the agency; the agencies, need to handle such issues in a professional way by means of a clearly defined process that is consistently applied. A complaints procedure allows an institution to state its dissatisfaction about the conduct of the process or those carrying it out.

In an appeals procedure, the institution questions the formal outcomes of the process, where it can demonstrate that the outcome is not based on sound evidence, that criteria have not been correctly applied or that the processes have not been consistently implemented.

Standards and guidelines for quality assurance agencies

Activities, policy and processes for quality assurance

Standard: Agencies normally undertake external quality assurance activities as defined in chapter 10 on a regular basis. They have clear and explicit goals and objectives that are part of their publicly available mission statement. These should translate into the daily work of the agency. Agencies should ensure the involvement of stakeholders in their governance and work.

Guidelines: To ensure the meaningfulness of external quality assurance, it is important that institutions and the public trust agencies.

Therefore, the goals and objectives of the quality assurance activities are described and published along with the nature of interaction between the agencies and relevant stakeholders in higher education, especially the higher education institutions, and the scope of the agencies' work. The expertise in the agency may be increased by including international members in agency committees.

A variety of external quality assurance activities are carried out by agencies to achieve different objectives. Among them are evaluation, review, audit, assessment, accreditation or other similar activities at programme or institutional level that may be carried out differently. When the agencies also carry out other activities, a clear distinction between external quality assurance and their other fields of work is needed.

Official status

Standard: Agencies should have an established legal basis and should be formally recognised as quality assurance agencies by competent public authorities.

Guidelines: In particular when external quality assurance is carried out for regulatory purposes, institutions need to have the security that the outcomes of this process are accepted within their higher education system, by the state, the stakeholders and the public.

Independence

Standard: Agencies should be independent and act autonomously. They should have full responsibility for their operations and the outcomes of those operations without third party influence.

Guidelines: Autonomous institutions need independent agencies as counterparts. In considering the independence of an agency the following are important: Organisational independence, demonstrated by official documentation (e.g. instruments of government, legislative acts or statutes of the organisation) that stipulates the independence of the agency's work from third parties, such as higher education institutions, governments and other stakeholder organisations; Operational independence: the definition and operation of the agency's procedures and methods as well as the nomination and appointment of external experts are undertaken independently from third parties such as higher education institutions, governments and other stakeholders; Independence of formal outcomes: while experts from relevant stakeholder backgrounds, particularly students, take part in quality assurance processes, the final outcomes of the quality assurance processes remain the re- sponsibility of the agency.

Anyone contributing to external quality assurance activities of an agency (e.g. as expert) is informed that while they may be nominated by a third party, they are acting in a personal capacity and not representing their constituent organisations when working for the agency. Independence is important to ensure that any procedures and decisions are solely based on expertise.

Thematic analysis

Standard: Agencies should regularly publish reports that describe and analyse the general findings of their external quality assurance activities.

Guidelines: In the course of their work, agencies gain information on programmes and institutions that can be useful beyond the scope of a single process, providing material for structured analyses across the higher education system. These findings can contribute to the reflection on and the improvement of quality assurance policies and processes in institutional, national and international contexts. A thorough and careful analysis of this information will show developments, trends and areas of good practice or persistent difficulty.

Resources

Standard: Agencies should have adequate and appropriate resources, both human and financial, to carry out their work.

Guidelines: It is in the public interest that agencies are adequately and appropriately funded, given higher education's important impact on the development of societies and individuals. The resources of the agencies enable them to organise and run their external quality assurance activities in an effective and efficient manner. Furthermore, the resources enable the agencies to improve, to reflect on their practice and to inform the public about their activities.

Internal quality assurance and professional conduct

Standard: Agencies should have in place processes for internal quality assurance related to defining, assuring and enhancing the quality and integrity of their activities.

Guidelines: Agencies need to be accountable to their stakeholders. Therefore, high professional standards and integrity in the agency's work are indispensable. The review and improvement of their activities are on-going so as to ensure that their services to institutions and society are optimal.

Agencies apply an internal quality assurance policy which is available on its website. This policy ensures that all persons involved in its activities are competent and act professionally and ethically; includes internal and external feedback mechanisms that lead to a continuous improvement within the agency; guards against intolerance of any kind or discrimination; outlines the appropriate communication with the relevant authorities of those jurisdictions where they operate; ensures that any activities carried out and material produced by subcontractors are in line with the NCHE, if some or all of the elements in its quality assurance activities are subcontracted to other parties; allows the agency to establish the status and recognition of the institutions with which it conducts external quality assurance.

Cyclical external review of agencies

Standard: Agencies should undergo an external review at least once every five years in order to demonstrate their compliance with the NCHE.

Guidelines: A periodic external review will help the agency to reflect on its policies and activities. It provides a means for assuring the agency and its stakeholders that it continues to adhere to the principles enshrined by NCHE.

Peer Review System for Quality Assurance Agencies

The system of peer review of agencies must include not only the peer review process itself, but also a careful consideration of the quality standards on which a review could build. Further, many academic commentators say that there must be the process that peer review of agencies should be interpreted as basically the means to achieve the goal of transparency, visibility and comparability of quality of agencies.

Experience elsewhere has shown that it is difficult to control such enterprises, but it takes expertise to have a unique opportunity to exercise practical management of this new market, not in order to protect the interests of already established agencies, but to make sure that the benefits of quality assurance are not diminished by the activities of disreputable practitioners. At the same time there has been awareness in the process that similar experiences and processes are developing internationally.

This chapter therefore opens with a brief analysis of the international experiences and initiatives relevant for the drafting of this part of the report. It then outlines the proposed peer review system based on the subsidiary principle and the Malawian standards for external quality assurance agencies. This outline leads to a presentation of the recommended register of external quality assurance agencies to operate in Malawi. The peer reviews and the agencies' compliance with the NCHE standards would play a crucial role in the composition of the register.

The reviews of agencies should include an assessment of whether the agencies are in compliance with the NCHE standards for external quality assurance agencies. The reviews should follow the process comprising a self-evaluation, an independent panel of experts and a published report.

An external review will typically be initiated at the national or agency level. It is therefore expected that reviews of agencies will usually follow from national regulations or from the internal quality assurance processes in place in the agency.

When national authorities initiate reviews, the purpose could obviously be quite broad and include the agency's fulfilment of the national mandate, e.g. However, it is a core element that reviews - regardless of whether they are initiated at a national or agency or must always explicitly consider the extent to which the agency conforms with the NCHE standards for external quality assurance agencies quality assurance agencies. Accordingly, the review of an agency will not only make evident the level of conformity with the NCHE standards, but also at the same time indicate the level of compliance with registration of membership criteria. Finally, the involvement of international experts with appropriate expertise and experience will provide substantial benefit to the review process. The register would meet the interest of higher education institutions and governments in being able to identify professional and credible quality assurance agencies operating in

Malawi. This interest has firstly its basis in the complicated area of recognition of non-national degrees. Recognition procedures would be strengthened if it were transparent to what extent providers were themselves quality assured by recognised agencies. Secondly, it is increasingly possible for higher education institutions to seek quality assurance from agencies across national borders. Higher education institutions would of course be helped in this process by being able to identify professional agencies from a reliable register.

The most valuable asset of the register would thus be its informative value to institutions and other stakeholders, and the register could in itself become a very useful instrument for achieving transparency and comparability of external quality assurance of higher education institutions. The register must make evident the level of compliance of entrants with the

European standards for external quality assurance agencies. However, it is important to stress that this report does not aim at proposing the register as a ranking instrument.

The register should be open for applications from all agencies providing services within Malawi. The agencies will be placed into different sections of the register depending on whether they are peer reviewed or not, whether they comply with the NCHE standards for external quality assur- ance agencies or not, and whether they operate strictly nationally or across borders.

International trends in Higher Education

Internationalisation Concept

The world of higher education is changing very fast, revolutionary (Altbach, 2010). Internationalization is one of the main drivers of change in HE- also in Africa (IAU,2010). In recent years the view has gained weight that the quality assessment of internationalisation policies and practices must not remain an specific activity of separate quality arrangements, but has to be integrated in the general quality assurance mechanisms of institutions and countries. In many cases, quality assurance procedures have been opened to include a review of internationalisation policies and prac- tices in institutions, and a review of programmes delivered in foreign countries, directly or in collaboration with domestic institutions abroad. The international dimension is becoming more important, complex and confusing (Knight, 2008)

What are the risks?

This is one of the main goals/drivers of internationalization. A way for international scholars to engage with global community. It is through collaborations that global inequalities can be re- duced. African universities have been part of the global higher education landscape since inception. The added value of international partnerships in growth of higher education has contributed to different activities-different outcomes. Partnerships have been characterized with unfairness with Africa not having her fair share. Africa for example is neither a key player nor very attractive partner...not seen as a priority region for future collaborations! Numerous barriers to engagement in global knowledge networks/societies have continued isolation.

Internationalisation of QA

Internationalisation and quality of higher education have always been closely linked together, at least at the conceptual level. This is based on the strong belief that internationalisation enhances the quality of higher education. Many policy documents, especially those published in the 1980s and early 1990s, consider internationalisation as a means to improving quality, rather than an end in itself. Examples include OECD (Organisation for Economic Co- operation and Development) and EU documents statements on national policies for internationalisation, and also many institutional-level policy plans for internationalisation.

From these various initiatives, it became clear that, although internationalisation and quality may be closely linked at a conceptual level, they were not so much linked at the level of practice and policy. Increased international competitiveness and international academic and professional mobility only had a marginal impact on the quality debates, which were situated at the level of national policy-making. Increasingly, quality assurance actors and agencies became involved in international networks and associations, e.g. the International Network of Quality Assurance Agencies in Higher Education (INQAAHE), through which they exchanged information and experiences. It was acknowledged that also in education, taking an international approach could strengthen quality assurance processes and outcomes, as had been the case for a time already in research reviews. Both external and internal pressures motivated the demand for international quality assurance. Internal pressures include the enhanced international mobility of students and the overseas marketing of higher education systems, i.e. the export of higher education, and external pressures come from the globalisation of the professions, regional trade agreements, and international organisations.

Internationalisation of quality assurance did not in all cases automatically lead to an increased focus on quality assurance of the increasingly important international dimension in higher education itself. The main reasons for this included: (a) internationalisation was in some cases still seen as a marginal activity (b) national processes for assuring quality were not intended to serve an international purpose (c) the diverse nature and spread of internationalisation activities within individual institutions and across institutions within a higher education system (d) the above- mentioned lack of co-ordination between quality assurance and internationalisation actors and agencies.

Transnational education: international quality assurance initiatives

Under the auspices of UNESCO (Europe region) and the Council of Europe and following the approval of the Convention on the Recognition of Qualifications concerning Higher Education in the European region (the Lisbon Convention). A Working Group on Transnational Education was set up (in 1998), to develop a Code of Good Practice in the Provision of Transnational Education. The composition of the Working Group reflected a mix of the education exporters, the USA, UK and Australia, countries where transnational education was delivered such as Israel, Slovakia and Spain, and countries that both receive and provide Transnational education such as Russia and Lat- via. The Code (which is still in draft) includes a set of principles that should be respected by institutions involved in the provision of educational services through transnational arrangements. The Code will be complemented by a recommendation on procedures and criteria for the assessment of foreign qualifications to be implemented by the network of recognition centres in the Europe region. See ESIB's TNE handbook for more information on this specific area of education.

Impact of internationalization of Education on Quality Assurance

The present nationalistic modes of quality assurance, including institutional and programmatic accreditation will inevitably have to work in conjunction and/or give way to global forms of public protection and educational quality. For serving the global market, it is important that the overall quality and standards of education available in a country must conform to certain thresh hold levels to become internationally acceptable. At the same time one has to realize that doing more or better of what one has been doing all along may not be enough to be accepted as international education. There must be a certain elements of educational provisions and the institutional basic infrastructure to make the grade as the provider of education for the international clientele. Many institutions are using several generic strategies for this purpose. Implementation of certain activities such as reorienting the curriculum focusing on the international needs and expectations, students and faculty exchanges, technical assistance from others to raise up beyond the national standards and having international students in the campuses to enhance the international ambience for the education they offer are some specific examples.

Likewise, emphasis on the development of new skills, knowledge, attitudes and values in students and faculty that will lead to the development of certain identified global/international competencies, promotion of international/intercultural activities in the campus must be given priority.

These may be implemented through either integration or infusion into teaching, research and services related activities. These initiatives should be backed up and supported by appropriate policies and processes at the institutional and/or at government level.

Nearly all the countries of the world have or in the process of developing quality assessment systems based on the four stage model of external evaluation of higher education, i.e., 1. A dedicated coordinating agency, 2. Submission of self-study and self-evaluation report by the institutions to the agency, 3. A peer review visit, usually on-site and 4. The preparation of a report accrediting on a two-point scale or on multi-point grade. Apparently, it would appear that this uniformity might provide a basis for a strong system of comparable quality assurance leading to the recognition of the studies and qualifications. However, there are many variations among countries in the details at each stage. Unless due emphasis is focused on the specific elements required to internationalize the higher education units, the outcomes of the national quality assurance mechanisms may not be indicative of the international quality. However, this should not be construed as implying that the national quality assessment is not important for each country. As of now, however the fact remains that most of the NQA agencies use the method that is not designed for assessing the elements that contribute to the international character of education provided.

Quality Assurance Framework for Universities in Malawi

Global and Domestic Forces

The content and delivery of higher education have been transformed in the last decade by a number of global and domestic forces. Those forces, which have impacted on and transformed higher education, including globalization, increasing new technologies in higher education and its delivery, massification of access to higher education and the entrance of market forces in higher education delivery. University education has shifted from being the preserve of the elite to a ser- vice open to the masses. By 2000, there were at least 80 million students worldwide taught by 3.5 million professionals in various categories of higher education institutions (World Bank 2000).

The number of University Institutions has also increased tremendously. In 1960, Africa had six universities, mainly producing graduates for employment as civil servants. Today, there are more than three hundred and fifty university institutions in Africa with more than half a million students. About thirty five percent of these institutions are private (i.e. non government). In Malawi there was only one university in 1993 (University of Malawi). To date there are about seventeen Universities in Malawi (Four Public Universities and Thirteen Private Universities) (NCHE). Giv- en this rapid expansion of higher education, some form of regulation is necessary to assure quality.

The Quality of Higher Education in Malawi

On one hand the increase in enrolments has created many problems foremost among them is a drop in quality. However, the establishment of National Council for Higher Education by the Act of Parliament No. 15 of 2011 has been timely if we look at the work the NCHE has demonstrated since its inception. NCHE is really doing commendable work. On the other hand in many institutions staff qualifications and experience are declining, there is little money for education inputs. Study areas such as classrooms, laboratories and libraries are overcrowded because of mismatch between student numbers and facilities. Staff salaries are low and there is little incentive for re- search. There is little money for the maintenance of the infrastructure and few institutions have comprehensive internal quality assurance mechanisms, Studies also indicate that most institutions have outdated curricula; encouraging memorization and not problem solving which indicates an orientation towards civil service employment. Furthermore, institutions have continued to expand enrolment despite lack of adequate facilities.

Though some institutions are good but many are not. The not so good has resorted to attempts to think that NCHE has come to bite so hard. Further, a number of foreign education service pro- viders have come on the market. Some deliver quality higher education but the majority have different goals and strategies from what Malawi's strategic plans are striving to achieve.

The Quality Assurance Framework

This Quality Assurance Framework in Malawi has been developed in an institutional, national, regional and international but rapid changing context. The aim of the framework is to ensure that NCHE and higher education institutions in Malawi work together to achieve and enhance the quality of higher education. The Quality Assurance Framework comprises of two major components: the regulatory component at the level of the NCHE and the institutional component at each individual university level.

Institutional and Programme Accreditation

Institutional accreditation or permitting Higher Education Institutions to exist and deliver higher education is a key tool of quality assurance. It is a process through which institutions are assessed at various stages before they are licensed or registered. It covers all aspects of institutions, including land, staffing, educational facilities, governance, financial resources and physical facilities. Additionally, it also includes the assessment of programmes.

In processing the applications for accreditation, the NCHE follows the provisions of thence Act (No. 15 of 2011) which gives mandate to the Council to make regulations to ensure provision of quality higher education.

According to the World Bank, accreditation is a process of self-study and external quality re- view that is used in higher education to scrutinize an institution and/or its programmes for quality standards and need for quality improvement. The process is designed to determine whether or not an institution has met or exceeded the published benchmark standards of quality (set by an external body such as a government, national quality assurance agency, or a professional association) for accreditation and is achieving its mission and stated purpose.

The process usually includes a self-evaluation, peer reviews and site visits. Success in this process results in the accreditation of a program or an institution. Both quality assurance and accreditation are new phenomena in most parts of the world. Thus, while in North America accreditation systems have existed for a long time now, in Europe they only came into being with the establishment of the Bologna Process in 1999.

In Africa the emergence of private higher education institutions triggered development of quality assurance agencies. Initially, the main purpose of quality assurance was to regulate private higher education institutions rather than to enhance accountability and improve quality. However, with time public universities and governments have recognized that quality assurance is an important tool to promote continuous quality improvement of universities so as to make them remain competitive nationally and internationally, to be accountable to the public, and to promote continuous innovativeness and reforms. Accreditation goes by various names, such as quality assurance, recognition, licensing etc. It is also considered as the major vehicle for external quality assurance or as a process of quality control and assurance in higher education, whereby as a result of inspection or assessment or both, an institution or its programmes and products there from (i.e. graduates, publications, etc.) are recognized as meeting minimum acceptable standards. Accreditation enables a Minister responsible for higher education or any other prescribed authority in a respective country to grant approval for an institution to operate as a higher education or professional institution, and to award recognized degrees or diplomas, hence giving the institution powers as a degree- granting authority.

Geographic Accreditation Worldwide, there are different arrangements of accreditation. These include those by countries or regions or similar groups of countries. An example of geographic accreditation arrangements may be cited for the United States of America (USA) where there are two types of accreditation, namely institutional and specialized accreditation. Institutional accreditation is granted by the regional and national accrediting agencies, which collectively serve most of the institutions that are chartered or licensed in the United States. These agencies only accredit total operating units. Specialized accreditation of professional or occupational institutions and programs is granted by national professional organizations in such fields as journalism, health sciences, engineering, law etc. In USA only the Department of Education (a governmental entity) and the Council for Higher Education Accreditation (which is non-governmental) are mandated to recognize the national systems of accreditation.

In Europe the process to harmonize the European higher education systems started in 1999 through the establishment of the Bologna Process. The aims of establishing the Bologna Process were to create a European Higher Education Area through harmonization of higher education, adopting a system of easily readable and comparable degrees, promoting mobility of both students and teachers, and promoting European co-operation in quality assurance in higher education. Although more than 46 European countries (both members and non-members of the European Union) are members of the Bologna Process, regional accreditation has not yet been established in Europe. So far accreditation in Europe is entrusted to one or more agencies in each country.

The European national accreditation agencies are often owned by - or at least approved by the government in the country where they operate. In most cases there is an arrangement that enables accreditation decisions in one country to be recognized in another country. Such system of recognition operates within the framework of the European Consortium for Accreditation in Higher Education, which was founded on a pan-European level in November 2003.

The Consortium was founded by twelve accreditation organizations from eight countries to help realize the European Higher Education Area by means of mutual recognition of accreditation decisions so as to promote greater mobility of students and staff, to inform the labor market on the values of degrees, and to contribute to the recognition of higher education credits and degrees within Europe. Three EAC Partner States (Kenya, Uganda and Tanzania) have also established a similar arrangement, which is facilitated through a memorandum of understanding signed in 2006. IUCEA subscribes to that arrangement. Similar arrangements also exist in other parts of the world, such as in Latin America and South East Asia. Regional accreditation requires the establishment of harmonized higher education systems, such as quality assurance and credit accumulation and transfer systems. This is indeed the case in USA, Europe and other regions where either regional accreditation systems exist or where there is mutual understanding such that accreditation decisions in one country are recognized in another country.

The Need for Regional Accreditation in East Africa For a long time now there have been discussions in the region focusing on the need to establish a regional system of accreditation in East Africa. To this effect, the East African Legislative Assembly (EALA) has gone further by coming up with a private member's motion to amend section 6 of the IUCEA Act, 2009 so as to empower IUCEA to accredit foreign university institutions operating in the EAC region. All along in these discussions IUCEA has continued to express its opinion regarding this move; that while the initiative is good since it will be part of implementation of harmonization of (higher) education in East Africa as EAC envisions, there are a number of issues that need to be addressed before it can be feasible. Additionally, IUCEA does not support setting up two parallel accreditation systems in the region, one for foreign universities and another one for local university institutions as the EALA member's private motion entails. Such arrangement will defeat the whole purpose of harmonizing the entire higher education system in the region. Actually, this will lead to the development of fragmented, parallel quality assurance systems for maintenance of the quality standards of university education in the region, i.e. one for local institutions under national accreditation systems and an- other one foreign university institutions under IUCEA. This may also have an overall negative effect on the quality of education in the region.

Some of the issues that need to be addressed so as to attain the establishment of systems for regional accreditation of university institutions and the education they provide in the region are as follows: a) Comprehensive amendment of the IUCEA Act 2009 so as to make IUCEA a truly EAC institution and not partly remaining an association of universities as it is currently the case; b) Establishment of a regional quality assurance framework that will guide the envisaged accreditation process to be implemented; c) Carrying out an IUCEA institutional review so as to make IUCEA a truly EAC institution by aligning the former's institutional structure to the operational structure of EAC, and to take into consideration IUCEA mandate, roles and functions as spelt out in the IUCEA Act 2009, as well as emerging issues including regional accreditation of university institutions; and d) Establishment of an appropriate legal linkage between national higher education commissions/ councils and IUCEA so as to harmonize national accreditation systems with those set regionally, and hence to avoid ambiguities and contradictions between national and regional systems of accreditation, or, alternatively to scrap the existing national accreditation systems, but no where in the world have national systems of accreditation been scrapped in favor of regional arrangements, most probably due to the need to maintain national interests and identity in higher education systems. IUCEA believes that while a regional accreditation system could be established, registration, licensing and chartering of university institutions should continue to be the prerogative of the individual Partner States, due to reasons stated in sections above.

IUCEA Efforts to Harmonize Higher Education Systems in East Africa Currently, quality assurance and accreditation systems in East Africa are handled at national level in each of the five EAC Partner States (Burundi, Kenya, Rwanda, Tanzania and Uganda), in accordance with the existing legal framework in each country. However, in order to promote regional collaboration in higher education as it has been the case since the era of the University of East Africa and later under the Inter- University Committee/ Inter-University Council for East Africa, higher education commissions/ councils in Uganda, Tanzania and Kenya have all along been working closely together in the area of their quality assurance and accreditation systems. Therefore, the current systems of accreditation are more or less harmonized, such that the accreditation status of an institution in one country is recognized in the other countries. Similarly, an institution registered in one Partner State can be allowed to operate in another country provided that the basic national requirements for it to operate in the other country have been met. In that regard, Kampala International University, which is registered and accredited in Uganda, has been allowed to operate in the other East African countries. Similarly, Jomo Kenyatta University of Agriculture and Technology (JKUAT), which is registered in Kenya, has been allowed to open a campus in Tanzania without being required to un- dergo another accreditation and chartering process in Tanzania.

IUCEA is aware that socio-economic trends fostered by globalization and the new world economic order has turned higher education into a tradable good. Thus, while higher education has continued to be a public entity, its delivery across geographic borders is no longer restrictive. Similarly, private (for profit) higher education providers continue to proliferate worldwide, including in East Africa. This has made it necessary to attach greater emphasis to higher education academic values in driving international competitiveness and cooperation in exchanging students, academic expertise and the labor force, and allowing foreign university institutions to operate in a particular country.

In this regard, emphasis continues to grow on the need for structured academic programmes and higher education systems that are responsive to the national, regional and international environment focused on: a) Promoting student and staff mobility among institutions and countries; b) Establishing appropriate systems of credit accumulation and transferability between institutions and beyond national boundaries; c) Adopting a system of easily readable, comparable and compatible qualifications within the country, region and globally; d) Promoting national and regional higher education dimensions through the evolvement of attractive regional higher education areas; e) Promoting lifelong learning and e-learning systems; f) Promoting accountability to stakeholders; g) Promoting graduate employability in the existing and emerging national, regional and international job market opportunities; and h) Promoting comparability of higher education quality standards and systems at national, regional and international levels.

These developments require appropriate systems that adhere to nationally, regionally and internationally recognized higher education benchmark standards, in the form of systematic quality assurance frameworks and accreditation systems. Therefore, since 2006 in collaboration with higher education commissions/councils in the EAC Partner States as well as member universities, IUCEA has been implementing a process to introduce a regional higher education quality assurance framework in East Africa that will facilitate international comparability, compatibility and competitiveness in the quality and relevance of university education delivered in the region. That process is well in an advanced stage and the needed operational instruments have already been developed in the form of a handbook.

The quality assurance framework is aimed at: Developing an East African higher education area; Enabling universities in the region to participate in cross-border education in and outside East Africa; Setting common higher education quality standards for East African university institutions as a process to facilitate mutual recognition of education and training systems, and qualifications and skills; Promoting and safeguarding comparability and compatibility of higher education standards and quality assurance processes in East Africa and beyond; Promoting graduate labor mobility regionally and internationally; and

Enhancing the drive towards the development of knowledge driven economies in the East African Community. Currently, a good number of university institutions as well as all the five national commissions/councils for higher education in each EAC Partner State are part of the process to establish the regional quality assurance framework. Furthermore, way back in 2007 a process to develop an East African credit transfer system was also initiated.

IUCEA has decided to follow up that initiative and accomplish it in the coming 2 - 3 years. Also IUCEA will soon initiate a process to develop a regional qualification framework that will aim at, among others, facilitating mutual recognition of qualifications among EAC Partner States so as to ease free movement of human capital in the region as envisioned in the EAC Common Market Protocol. Meanwhile, IUCEA is finalizing an institutional review process, aimed at making IUCEA a truly EAC institution by aligning the former's institutional structure to the operational structure of EAC, and to take into consideration IUCEA mandate, roles and functions as spelt out in the IUCEA Act 2009, as well as emerging issues including the possibility for introducing re- gional accreditation of university institutions.

The initiatives that IUCEA is taking are important preparatory frameworks for the possibility of eventual establishment of a regional system of accreditation of higher education in the region. In that regard, IUCEA has been working and will continue to work closely with higher education commissions/councils in the EAC Partner States and professional bodies in the region so as to arrive at a common understanding for the establishment of a harmonized higher education framework for East Africa, encompassing commonly accepted quality assurance and benchmark standards, and accreditation processes.

This will also require an overhaul of the current Inter- University Council for East Africa Act 2009 and extensive review of the IUCEA institutional structure so as to make IUCEA not only a strategic institution of EAC responsible for the coordination of human resource and research development in the region, but also to make it a legal entity responsible for handling quality assurance and accreditation systems for the regional, in a manner that will be determined by the EAC Partner States. IUCEA is already working towards this direction. It is expected that a comprehensive framework in this process will have been established by the end of June 2012.

Academic Programmes

According to NCHE (2014:5) the institution may, in special circumstances start a programme of study and seek accreditation later, provided that: provisional approval is granted by the Council before students are accepted into the programme and the programme is accredited before the students graduate.

The institution must ensure that the academic programmes are consistent with and serve to fulfil its mission and purposes. The institution should work systematically and effectively to plan, provide, oversee, evaluate, improve and assure the academic quality and integrity of its academic programmes and the credits and degrees awarded or to be awarded. The institution is also expected to set a standard of student achievement appropriate to the degree awarded and develops the systematic means to understand how and what students are learning and to use the evidence obtained to improve the academic programmes (NCHE 2014).

The institution must also ensure that each educational programme demonstrates coherence through its goals, structure and content; policies and procedures for admission and retention; instructional methods and procedures; and the nature, quality and extent of student learning and achievement. NCHE (2014) also says the institution offering multiple academic programmes must ensure that all programmes meet or exceed the basic quality standards of the institution and that there is reasonable consistence in quality among them. Additionally, the institution must ensure that students use information resources and information technology as an integral part of their education. It provides appropriate orientation and training foe use of these resources as well as instructional and support in information literacy and information technology appropriate to the level and field of study.

When programmes are eliminated or programme requirements are changed the institution should make appropriate arrangements for enrolled students so that they may complete their education with a minimum of disruption.

At all levels the institution is also expected to provide sufficient resources to sustain and improve each of its programmes. To this end the institution should allocate resources on the basis of its academic planning, need and objectives.

Undergraduate Degree Programmes

NCHE (2014) points out that undergraduate programmes are designed to give students a substantial and coherent introduction to the broad areas of human knowledge, their theories and methods of inquiry, plus in-depth study in at least one disciplinary interdisciplinary area. Programmes have an appropriate rationale. Students successfully completing an undergraduate programme demonstrate competence in written and oral communication in English; the ability to engage in scientific and quantitative reasoning, critical analysis and logical thinking; and the capability for continuing learning, including the skills of information literacy. They also demonstrate knowledge and understanding of scientific, historical and social phenomena, and a knowledge and appreciation of the aesthetic dimensions of humankind.

Postgraduate Degree Programmes

According to NCHE (2014) postgraduate degree programmes are designed to give students a mastery of a complex field of study or professional area. Programmes have an appropriate rationale; their clarity and order are visible in stated requirements, in relevant official publications and in the demonstrated learning experiences of graduates. Learning objectives reflect a high level of complexity, specialization and generalization. Postgraduate programmes are not offered unless resources and expectations exceed those required for an undergraduate programme in a similar field.

Institutions who aspire to offer postgraduate degrees must have an adequate staff of full time faculty in areas appropriate to the degree offered, or have made arrangements with qualified adjunct/part time staff, Academic staff responsible for postgraduate programmes must have appropriate credentials, experience and time commitment for the successful accomplishment of programme objectives and programme or improvement. The scholarly expectations of academic staff exceed those expected for staff working at the undergraduate level. Research oriented programmes have an adequate number of active research scholars on their faculties. Professionally-oriented programmes include experienced professionals on faculty, who are making scholarly contributions to the devel- opment of the field. Students admitted to postgraduate degree programmes are demonstrably quali- fied for advanced academic study.

Degree requirements of the institution's postgraduate programmes take into account specific programmes purposes. Research-oriented programmes, including the Ph.D. and master's degree programmes should be designed to prepare students for scholarly careers; they should emphasise acquisition, organization, utilization and dissemination of knowledge. Doctoral degree programmes should afford the student substantial mastery of the subject matter, theory, literature and methodology of a significant of study. They include a sequential development of research skills leading to the attainment of an independent research capacity.

Students should undertake original research that contributes to new knowledge in the chosen field of study. Master's programmes have many of the same objectives but require less sophisticated levels of mastery in the chosen field of study than does the research doctorate. While they need not require students to engage in original research, they do provide an understanding of research appropriate to the discipline and the manner in which it is conducted.

Measures for Quality Assurance at Institutional Level

Institutions are primary responsible for quality and quality management. Each University will have an independent quality assurance unit that sets quality assurance control guidelines in the University and that continuously reviews all programmes, teaching and assessment. The responsibility of NCHE is to establish value adding systems of external valuation which can validate the institutional information on effectiveness of internal quality arrangements. The NCHE will use peer and expert reviews to conduct external audits in a regular assessment.

Institutional Audits

Institutional audits are the core of the institutional quality assurance framework. The NCHE will, at regular intervals, undertake external audits to assess the capacity of institutions for quality management taking into account their missions, goals and objectives. The institutions will undertake internal institutional audits and participate in external institutional audits.

The main objectives of the institutional and external audits are to:

- ☐ Encourage higher education providers to cultivate and maintain a culture of continuous performance improvement
- ☐ Enable institutions to develop reliable quality assurance performance indicators to assure stakeholders and the NCHE that the policies, strategies and resources for delivery of quality higher education
- ☐ Validate self evaluation reports
- ☐ Provide information to all stakeholders on the strength and weaknesses of the institution
- ☐ According to NCHE (2014) after every five years, higher education institutions in Malawi will be required to undergo the external audits.

Institutional Audits Criteria

The NCHE in Malawi has identified areas to examine or evaluate in institutional audits as spelled out below:

Institutional Governance

Well government institutions have strong "institutionality", with functioning structures like the University Council, Senate, Faculties, Departments and Unions whose powers are well defined. A well governed institution does not only depend on the charisma or the strength of a leader but rather on its own institutional strengths embedded in its structures, traditions, rules, achievements and availability.

The Quality of Teaching and Learning

Internal and external auditors shall use the following benchmarks to assess the quality levels of teaching and learning:

- ☐ Implementation of NCHE regulations on standards
- ☐ Adherence to or improving of the minimum requirement of courses of study issued by the NCHE
- ☐ Relevance of what is taught for the job market and the nation
- ☐ Methods of examining or assessing of students, including examination regulations and awards
- ☐ Quality of graduates, if necessary measured against the quality of entering students
- ☐ Appeal mechanisms for students
- ☐ Protection of unique and professional programme against general polcies that may not apply to all disciplines
- ☐ Access to information by students in the following unit: Libraries, Computer Labs and internet access
- ☐ The Quality of Academic Staff
- ☐ The quality of academic staff is key to the quality of a University. Auditors of the Universties shall review the following:
- ☐ The regulations regarding the appointment, promotion and dismissal of staff
- ☐ Recruitment Policies and use of part time lectures
- ☐ Staff/student ratios in various programmes
- ☐ Student's assessments of academic staff and their usefulness in improving teaching performance in Quality Assurance Regulations.

Sufficiency of Education Facilities

Auditors shall review education facilities to establish whether or not they comply with NCHE requirements. Special attention shall be paid to:

- ☐ Access to relevant and up-to0date texts and other books as well as articles in journals
- ☐ Access to computer networks and the Internet

- ☐ Access to general education equipment, including power point projectors, slide projectors, overhead projectors, video, video cameras, television sets, public address systems among others
- ☐ Access to sports and recreation facilities a
- ☐ Student exchange programmes to enhance student experiences

Research and Publication

Universities are supposed to be centres of research, academic excellence, scholarships, knowledge generation and publications. Institutional auditors shall assess the quality of research and knowledge creation of a given institution. The institution shall monitor and periodically evaluates the sufficiency and support for the academic staff and the effectiveness of the academic staff in teaching and advising, research and scholarship as appropriate to institutional mission, research and creative activity. The results of these evaluations are used to enhance fulfilment of the institution's mission.

The Quality Output

- ☐ The auditors will measure outputs from the University including but not limited to, quality of graduates, quality of research and publications and the performance of alumni in the job market. Institution auditors shall examine the following areas in order to determine the quality of outputs of a given University institution.
- ☐ The period it takes graduates of a given institution to get full employment after graduation
- ☐ The existence of a system of "tracing" where graduates go. The system of how graduates are followed up and tracked after completing their studies in a given University
- ☐ Research, publications, patent registration, consultancies and other awards obtained by staff and students of a given University
- ☐ The duration the students take to graduate

Institutional Financial Management (Financial Resources)

Given the centrality of financial management in the delivery and sustenance of quality higher education the auditors shall be interested to examine the following: The budget process, sources funding such as Government, where applicable; fees; endowments or Donors and development partners. Therefore the University shall ensure that the intuition's resources are sufficient to sustain the quality of its educational programmes and to support institutional improvement now and in the foreseeable future. The institution provides adequate evidence of its financial capacity to graduate its entering class. To this end the institution must administer its financial resources with integrity.

It is important that the institution manages its financial resources and allocates them in a way that reflects its mission and purposes. It preserves and enhances available financial resources sufficient to support its mission. It demonstrates the ability to respond to financial emergencies and unforeseen circumstances.

Integrity of the Academic Qualification

The institution's degrees and other forms of academic recognition are appropriately named, following practices common are to the National Qualifications Framework in terms of length, con- tent and level of the programmes. It is important that the institution demonstrates its clear and ongoing authority and administrative oversight for the academic elements of all courses for which it awards institutional credit or credentials. These responsibilities include time required for course content and the delivery of the instructional programme; contact hours, selection, approval, profession development and evaluation of faculty, admission, registration and retention of students; evaluation of prior learning, and evaluation of student progress, including the award and recording of credit. The institution retains systems and structures as well as responsibility for the academic credit or degrees are awarded, even with contractual or other arrangement.

The level of awards should be consistent with Council policy and the course content, appropriate to the field of study and the course content, appropriate to the field of study and reflect the level and amount of student learning. The levels of awards are based on policies developed and overseen by the academic and administrative staff.

The institution should also ensure that graduation requirements are clearly stated in appropri- ate electronic and print publications and are consistently applied in the degree certification process. The degrees awarded accurately reflect attainments

Library and Other Information Resources

The institution must ensure that it has sufficient and appropriate library and information resources. It ensures adequate access to these resources and demonstrates their effectiveness in fulfilling its mission. It provides instructional and information technology sufficient to support its teaching, learning and research environment.

The institution must plan and allocate resources that will support the development of library, information resources and technology appropriate to the institution's mission and academic programmes. The institution must provide sufficient and consistent financial support for the library and the effective maintenance and improvement of instruction's information resources and instructional and information technology. The institution should use instructional and information technology appropriate to its academic mission and the modes of delivery of its academic programmes.

Faculty, staff and students should be provided appropriate training and support to make effective use of library and information resources and instructional and information technology. The institution should also ensure that appropriate access to library and information resources and services for all students regardless of programme location or mode of delivery, taking into account students with disabilities.

The institution is expected to ensure that students have available and are appropriately directed to sources of information appropriate to support and enrich their academic work and adequate numbers of professionally qualified staff administer the institutuon "a library, information resources and services and instructional and information technology support functions.

Physical and Technology infrastructure and Resources

The institution must ensure that it has sufficient and appropriate physical and technological infrastructure and resources necessary for the achievement of its purposes and that it manages and maintains the infrastructure and resources in a manner to sustain and enhance the realization of institutional goals.

The institution's physical and technological infrastructure and resources, including classrooms, laboratories, network infrastructure, materials, equipment and buildings and grounds, whether owned or rented are commensurate with institutional purposes. To this end they must be designed, maintained and managed at both on and off campus sites in a manner that serves institutional needs. Proper management, maintenance and operation of all physical facilities, including student housing provided by the institution, are accomplished by adequate and competent staffing.

It is also important to ensure that classrooms and other facilities are appropriately equipped and adequate in capacity. Classrooms and other teaching spaces should support teaching methods appropriate to the discipline. Students and academic staff, including those with disabilities have access to appropriate physical, technological and educational resources to support teaching, learning and research.

Institutions should also ensure that facilities are constructed and maintained in accordance with legal requirements to ensure access, safety, security and a healthful environment, with consideration for environmental and ecological concerns.

Public Disclosure

The institution must ensure that in presenting itself to students, prospective students and other members of the interested public, the institution provides information that is complete, accurate, timely, accessible, clear and sufficient for intended audiences to make informed decisions about the institution.

The information published by the institution, including on its website, should be sufficient to allow students and prospective students to make informed decisions about their education. The institution's public website should include the information specified elsewhere in this section.

The institution should inform the public of the information available about itself and how inquiries can be addressed. It must also be responsive to reasonable requests for information about itself. The institution should also provide notice as to the availability upon request of its publications and its most recent audited financial statements or a fair summary thereof.

The Licensing Process

As stated in chapter 1 the National Council for Higher Education (NCHE) was established by Act of Parliament No. 15 of 2011, with the primary purpose of providing accreditation and quality assurance services in higher education institutions. Specifically, the NCHE aims to promote and coordinate education provided by higher education institutions, design quality assurance systems and determine, maintain and regulate standards for teaching, examinations, qualifications and facilities; register, de-register and accredit higher education institutions; determine framework for funding higher education and provide guidance on terms and conditions for awarding students' grants, loans and scholarships; and harmonize student selection into public higher education institutions.

Two types of accreditation are available:

First, the Institutional Accreditation i.e., for a higher education as a whole or for its structural units. Second, the Program Accreditation. However, there are three accreditation categories:

1. **Accredited:** Indicates that the higher education institution or the study programmes meets the set of requirements. The decision may also include recommendations for eliminating minor shortcomings.
2. **Conditionally Accredited:** Indicates than institution or study program under Review has major shortcomings, which need to be eliminated or addressed.
3. **Not Accredited:** Indicates that the institution or study program has serious shortcomings that jeopardize the quality of graduates knowledge and skills. In the case of a negative accreditation decision ("Not Accredited") for the first time for an institution

or study program, the university/ applied higher education institution may apply for a second accreditation, one year after the first accreditation decision.

Experience shows that accreditation of the curriculum means the accreditation for the institution, particularly if the curriculum, which was accredited, is the profile course for this institution. The awareness of students about accreditation has grown but it is troubling that the students don't believe that their opinions are considered in the process. Their knowledge is also lacking on the part that accreditation is a continuous process aimed at improvement. Accreditation processes have stimulated inner quality assessment at the university, faculty and department level to the extent that there is a goal to establish a regular quality assurance system within the university. This would be a beneficial addition to the overall quality management model. In this respect quality management would lead to quality improvement.

www.ingramcontent.com/pod-product-compliance
Lightning Source LLC
Chambersburg PA
CBHW030913180526
45163CB00004B/1811